Plato's *Republic*
An Introduction

Sean Sayers

Edinburgh University Press

© Sean Sayers, 1999
Edinburgh University Press
22 George Square, Edinburgh

Typeset in Ehrhardt and Futura
by Bibliocraft Ltd, Dundee, and
printed and bound in Great Britain
by MPG Books Ltd, Bodmin

A CIP record for this book is available
from the British Library

ISBN 0 7486 1188 6 (paperback)

Contents

Preface

The *Republic* was written more than 2000 years ago, yet it continues to be one of the most widely read books in the whole literature of philosophy. It is still the work through which many are first introduced to the subject. Students are often apprehensive at the prospect of having to study it. They fear it will be boring and irrelevant. Few find it so. On the other hand, many are shocked and repelled by its authoritarian and illiberal attitudes, and fail to see beyond these to its deeper philosophical themes – themes which are more likely to engage their sympathy and interest. My main purpose in this book is to bring out these philosophical themes and to locate them in the context of contemporary debates.

It is remarkable that such an ancient work can still be read in this way: philosophically, for its ideas. But it would not have surprised Plato. According to his Theory of Forms, philosophy expresses eternal truths about a timeless subject matter. Whether and in what respects this theory is true is discussed below at length. Even granted that it is true, however, we can appropriate Plato's ideas only in our own terms and in our own context. His philosophy is kept alive by being translated and discussed, reproduced and recreated, by each successive generation in its own way and in its own terms.

This is a continual process; but it is particularly called for at present. During the last half century or so discussion of the *Republic* has been inextricably bound up with the Cold War and its divisions. A succession of influential commentators has treated the utopian society that Plato describes either as the initial blueprint for Soviet communism (Crossman, Popper) or as an early warning against it (Strauss, Bloom). In either case, Plato has been recruited as a main participant in the ideological battle between such communism and the liberal, individualist, free market philosophy of the 'Free World'.

At times the polemical purpose of these accounts compromises their scholarly and philosophical value. Thus Popper sometimes seems incapable of distinguishing Plato's republic from the Soviet Union, and he attacks Plato by appealing to notions of democracy and individual rights which would have been incomprehensible to Plato or his contemporaries. Nevertheless, these writers are not wrong to treat Plato as an ancestor of socialism. In particular, as we shall see, Plato presents – with a clarity that has never been surpassed – the fundamental tenets of a utopian and communitarian view of society. These are essential aspects of the socialist outlook and the main alternative to liberal individualism.

With the collapse of Soviet communism the context of political debate has changed dramatically. Plato's ideas must now be reassessed free from the constraints imposed by the antagonisms of the Cold War. This book is a contribution to that process. One of its aims is to reinterpret the *Republic* in the context of the post-Cold War world.

It is sometimes said that the collapse of Soviet communism signifies the permanent triumph of capitalism and liberal democracy – the 'end of history' no less – and with this the end of all utopian social dreams. If that turns out to be true then Plato's philosophy will indeed have been refuted and finally laid to rest. But there are no valid grounds to believe this will happen – at least, that is the conviction with which this book is written. The troubles and conflicts created by individual self-interest upon which Plato focuses in his philosophy are still present, in forms far more intense than anything that Plato could have envisaged. They are endemic to capitalist society. Plato's critique is as relevant today as it was when it was first composed, at the dawn of commercial society. Utopian hopes for a harmonious community and a better world are as keenly felt as ever. There is no good reason to think that they are doomed and that we are at the end of history. Even in these bleak times forces of criticism and opposition still exist; and, properly understood, Plato's philosophy continues to be a source of illumination and strength for them.

One of the main features of Plato's philosophy is its systematic character. This is most evident in the *Republic*. Though its focus is primarily on moral and social issues, it relates these to central topics in education, the philosophy of art and literature, the theory of knowledge, metaphysics and logic. I cover Plato's views in all these areas. However, I keep my focus firmly on the *Republic* and refer to other dialogues only to throw light on this work. My aims throughout are twofold: first, to explain Plato's philosophy in the *Republic* and to locate his ideas in the context of current debates; and second to assess critically this philosophy by defending it where possible and criticising it where not. In this way I seek to provide an introductory philosophical commentary to this great work.

A number of good modern translations of the *Republic* are currently available with little to choose between them. I quote mainly from Lee's Penguin translation (variations are noted). Reference to the *Republic* and to other works of Plato is made to the standard Stephanus edition page numbers which are to be found in the margins of most editions.

I depart from the standard translations in a couple of ways which should be noted. Plato's topic is not a 'republic' in the modern sense, but rather the *polis* or ancient Greek city state. There is no precise equivalent for this term in modern English. It is usually translated either as 'state' (Lee, Cornford) or 'city' (Bloom). Neither is entirely satisfactory. On the one hand, 'state' is too specifically political in its modern usage to capture the generality of Plato's meaning. On the other hand, 'city' sounds too archaic. The reader is constantly reminded that Plato is writing about a very different sort of society. In certain contexts this may be helpful; but when one is reading Plato philosophically the aim is rather to see it in relation to contemporary circumstances and issues. If Plato had been writing today he would probably have talked about 'society'. For the most part this is the term I employ.

Much of Plato's discussion concerns the individual self. The Greek word he uses is *psuchē* (the root of the English words 'psyche', 'psychology', etc.). It is standardly translated as 'soul', but the Greek has no particularly religious, spiritual or even specifically mental connotations. Thus for Aristotle *psuchē* is simply what animates the matter of any living organism: all living things have a 'soul', even plants.[1] For this reason I shall generally use the terms 'self' or 'personality' instead.

---

[1] *Ethics* 1102a–b.

Acknowledgements

My understanding of the *Republic* has developed over many years of teaching. I am grateful to generations of students in a variety of courses for helping me to clarify my thoughts. I am also grateful to a number of people for their criticisms of earlier drafts, including particularly Simon Glendinning, Joseph McCarney, David McLellan, John O'Neill, Scott Meikle, Janet Sayers, Anne Seller, Tony Skillen and Barry Willcox. I owe a special debt of gratitude to my colleague, Richard Norman, from whose teaching of moral and social philosophy in general and Plato in particular I have learned a great deal over the years, and who has read and commented in detail on this work through all the stages of its preparation.

Canterbury
September 1998

1 Plato and the *Republic*

Plato was born in about 427 BC and died in 347 BC, aged about 80, in Athens. Greece was then made up of a number of small, autonomous city states (*poleis*, singular: *polis*), of which Athens was the most powerful and prosperous. Its power and wealth were based upon commerce and trade. After the defeat of the Persians in the great naval battle of Salamis in 480 BC Athens had become the dominant maritime power in the region. Under the leadership of Pericles, in the mid fifth Century, Athens reached its greatest splendour as a political, cultural and intellectual centre.

Just before Plato was born, however, Athens went into dramatic decline. She became embroiled in the Peloponnesian War, the long struggle with Sparta for supremacy in the region. After a succession of military defeats, this eventually ended in 404 BC with the downfall of Athens and its subjection by Sparta. The strain of these defeats led to political instability. There was a series of coups and counter-coups. Democratic, oligarchic and tyrannical regimes followed each other in rapid succession.

Plato grew up in this period of instability and decline. There is little reliable information about his early life. His parents both came from wealthy and powerful aristocratic families with important political connections. It would have been natural for Plato to have entered politics. If the autobiographical seventh *Letter* is to be believed he wished to do so but a number of factors made him hesitate.[1]

---

[1] The authenticity of *Letter* VII has been doubted. However, it originates so closely in time to Plato that it is likely to be an accurate record of at least the main details of his life.

When I was a young man I expected, like many others, to embark, as soon as I was my own master, on a political career. The condition in which I found public affairs was this. People were dissatisfied with the existing constitution, and a revolution took place [the oligarchic revolution of the 'Thirty Tyrants' in 404 BC] ... Some of [the leaders] were relations and acquaintances of mine and invited me at once to join them in what seemed an obvious career for me. Naturally enough, in view of my youth, I expected that this government would bring about a change from corrupt to upright administration, and I watched with the keenest interest to see what they would do. I found that it had taken these men no time at all to make the previous government look like an age of gold.[2]

The 'Thirty Tyrants' were soon overthrown, but the outlook changed little. As a young man, Plato had come under the influence of the teacher and philosopher Socrates, who was about 40 years Plato's senior. Socrates was evidently an extraordinary person. He wrote nothing, yet his ideas have exerted an influence second to none on western thought. What we know of his character and ideas comes from the writings of his disciples and contemporaries. He is the main figure in many of Plato's dialogues, where he is portrayed as a figure of unshakable moral integrity. He also features in works by the historian and writer Xenophon and he is satirised by the playwright Aristophanes in his comedy *The Clouds*.

In 399 BC, Socrates was tried and executed for corrupting the youth of Athens. To Plato this charge was absurd and monstrous – a sign of the rotten state of Athenian politics.

When I saw ... the kind of men who were active in politics and the principles on which things were managed, I concluded that it was difficult to take part in public life and retain one's integrity, and this feeling became stronger the more I observed and the older I became ... so that I, who began by being full of enthusiasm for a political career, ended by growing dizzy at the spectacle of universal confusion. I did not cease to consider how an improvement might be effected in this particular situation and in politics in general, and I remained on the watch for the right moment for action.[3]

In Athens, this moment was never to arrive. After the death of Socrates, Plato turned increasingly to writing and philosophy,

[2] *Letter* VII 324.
[3] *Letter* VII 325–6.

though he did not entirely abandon thoughts of a more active political role.

> Finally I came to the conclusion that the condition of existing states is bad – nothing can cure their constitutions but a miraculous reform assisted by good luck – and I was driven to assert, in praise of true philosophy, that nothing else can enable one to see what is right for states and for individuals, and that the troubles of mankind will never cease until either true and genuine philosophers attain political power or the rulers of states by some dispensation of providence become genuine philosophers.[4]

This is the central political thesis of the *Republic*. In the hope of being able to put his political ideas into practice Plato made three visits to Syracuse, a Greek colony in Sicily, at the invitation of its rulers. But these hopes came to nothing and Plato was forced to flee.

He returned to Athens where he finally abandoned the idea of a political career and turned to teaching and writing. In 386 BC he founded the Academy, a school for the philosophical training of statesmen, and one of the first institutions of higher education in the western world. This was to be the centre of his activity during the second half of his long life. Its most celebrated pupil was Aristotle, who came at the age of 17 and remained until Plato's death, twenty years later.

Numerous works by Plato have survived down to the present-day. They almost all take the form of dialogues in which Socrates is in debate with various other, often real and identifiable, figures. For example, Glaucon and Adeimantus in the *Republic* are Plato's older brothers. Moreover, the dialogues are often set in realistic surroundings, and the participants are vividly portrayed as real individuals with great literary and dramatic skill (e.g., Thrasymachus in the *Republic*). However, Plato's primary purpose is not to record actual encounters or to portray real individuals. The participants are presented rather as the ideal representatives of different philosophical positions.

This is true also of the portrayal of Socrates. It is possible that we get a more or less faithful account of Socrates' methods and ideas in the earlier dialogues. In these Socrates puts forward no doctrine of his own, but critically questions the views of his interlocutors (as in

---

[4] *Letter* VII 326.

Book I of the *Republic*). However, the approach changes in Plato's later works (and in later books of the *Republic*). Socrates is increasingly made to assert a positive position of his own, and the dialogue form is used simply to break up his speeches. To what extent these express views that are those of the historical Socrates and to what extent they are specifically Plato's is a subject of much speculation. Even though Socrates remains the central voice in Plato's dialogues, it seems likely that Plato increasingly used it to express his own distinctive philosophy as time went on.

In particular, the idea of a separate world of intelligible forms and the belief in an immortal soul are thought to be specific to Plato. Both doctrines are prominent in the *Republic*. It is likely that it was composed towards the middle of Plato's career as a writer (around 375 BC) in the early years of the Academy, for which the section on the higher education of the Guardians in Book VII perhaps gives a sketch of the curriculum. However, it is not ultimately possible to determine what in Plato's work is derived from Socrates and what is contributed by Plato himself, and I shall not attempt to do so. In what follows I shall generally attribute the ideas of the *Republic* to Plato.

The Republic

The *Republic* is one of the most influential and widely read works in the whole of western philosophy. At first sight, this is surprising. Plato explains his ideas by describing a utopia, an ideal society. He maintains that this ideal is a timeless expression of pure reason. In many respects, however, it is clearly derived from and rooted in the social conditions of its time.

It is important to realise that when Plato talks of a 'republic', 'state', 'city' or 'society' it is a city state or *polis* on the ancient Greek model to which he is referring. This was something quite different from the modern nation state. It was a small self-governing community, comprising a city and its surrounding area: a predominantly agrarian society, based upon slavery, in which the family-household was the main economic and social unit.

In an earlier period, Athens had been ruled by a king and elders along the lines portrayed in Homer. By the fifth century it had evolved into a democracy. Plato is bitterly critical of these changes and harks back to earlier times: he is a conservative thinker, even by the standards of his own time. However, what he is attacking must not be confused with modern, representative democracy. The ancient Athenian variety was quite different. It was a participatory form of government. Authority was exercised directly through an assembly of all citizens. However, not all adult inhabitants were citizens; indeed the majority – women, slaves and foreigners – were excluded.

In Plato's time Athenian society was changing rapidly. Traditional customs and institutions were being undermined by the new forces of trade and commerce. Accepted values and ideas were being widely questioned and criticised. There was an unprecedented explosion of speculative and critical thought about all things. The Presocratics and the Sophists, as well as Socrates, Plato and Aristotle, all emerge in this period, which is known as the Greek enlightenment and which sees the birth of philosophy. Plato is a part of this movement, even while he sets himself in opposition to many of the changes then occurring. It is too simple to see him merely as a reactionary who opposes all change in order to preserve the 'closed', 'tribal' society of the past against the 'open' democratic society emerging in Athens.[5]

Sparta was a very different sort of society. It often serves Plato as a model. It lacked access to the sea. It was less affected by commercial forces and had remained a more traditional society than Athens. It was a highly militaristic society in which a great degree of conformity and uniformity was enforced. Dress and manners were austere and simple. Nevertheless, mainly because of its military success, Sparta was regarded as a model by many Athenians, including Plato. His picture of the ideal society in the *Republic* incorporates a number of its features; although he also criticises some of its aspects under the name of 'timarchy' (545c–548d).

Structure of the Argument

The central topic of the *Republic* is the nature of justice. 'Justice' is the usual translation of the Greek word *dikaiosunē*. As Plato uses it, this word has a wider meaning than its modern English equivalent:

[5] K. R. Popper, *The Open Society and Its Enemies*, Vol. I, Ch. 10.

it refers not just to questions of legal and political right, but also to moral issues. This broad usage is reflected in the wide scope of the argument of the *Republic*. The book deals not only with social and political issues, but equally with moral and psychological ones. Indeed, a fundamental theme of the book is that these two kinds of questions cannot be dealt with apart. For human beings, Plato maintains, are social creatures who can live well only in some form of community with others. And questions about the right way for the individual to live are thus for Plato ultimately inseparable from questions about the right form of society.

The structure of the *Republic* is complex and not immediately apparent. Nevertheless, a single line of argument is pursued throughout the work. The traditional division of the text into ten books is arbitrary and gives no guide to this. It was determined more by the constraints of book production in the ancient world than by the logic of the intellectual content, the size of a book being set by the amount of writing that could be fitted onto a sheet of papyrus. While reference to the old books is now so well established as to be unavoidable, modern editors of the text often introduce their own more logical divisions which vary only slightly from editor to editor. The structure of the argument can best be understood, I believe, in terms of the following main divisions.

Introduction: the challenge to Socrates (I.327a–II.367e). This section introduces the central question to be addressed in the *Republic*: what is justice and how can it be realised in society and in individual life? This question is first raised in Book I through Socrates' encounters with Cephalus, Polemarchus and Thrasymachus, who represent common and typical attitudes towards morality and justice. Then Glaucon and Adeimantus challenge Socrates to show that justice is good not only for its external rewards but also in itself (Chapter 2).

Justice in society and in the individual (II.367e–V.449a). Plato gives a first answer to the question, 'what is justice?', by outlining his basic assumptions about human nature and society (Chapter 3). He then describes the ideal society, with particular stress on the education of its future rulers (Chapter 4). Justice, he argues, resides in the harmonious functioning of the community as a whole (chapters 5–6). Plato then develops an analogy between the social order and the individual self. Justice in the individual consists analogously in the harmonious functioning of the individual self (Chapter 7).

Appendix: 'Communism' and the role of women (V.449a–471c). In the first part of what is presented as a lengthy 'digression', Plato defends his 'communistic' proposals that the rulers of his ideal society should have no private property, that their families should be abolished and that women should be equal with men (Chapters 5 and 8).

The Theory of Forms and higher education (V.471c–VII.541b). The 'digression' is extended to justify the central political idea of the dialogue: that justice can be achieved only when society is governed by 'philosophers' according to rational principles (philosophy for Plato encompasses the whole of rational knowledge) (Chapter 9). To explain the nature of rational knowledge Plato introduces the idea of a realm of intelligible forms separate from the world of the senses. He then describes the process of higher education which leads to a knowledge of this realm. Only reason, Plato maintains, can give true knowledge of justice and other values, and hence reliable guidance about how to arrange human social and individual life. This constitutes a second and, Plato believes, deeper account of the nature of justice in terms of the Theory of Forms (Chapters 10–11).

The reply to the Sophists (VIII.543a–IX.592b). The main thread of the argument is resumed after the lengthy digression. The argument now takes a negative form. Plato's focus turns to imperfect and unideal societies in order to demonstrate that when reason and philosophy are not the ruling principles in society and the individual self, the result is injustice and unhappiness. Just and unjust lives are compared in order to show that justice is valuable in itself. Thus Plato responds to the initial challenge (Chapter 12).

Appendix: the attack on poetry and the immortality of the soul (X.595a–621d). This section seems like an addendum to the main argument. It is made up of two unconnected parts. In the first, Plato returns to the subject of poetry, already discussed in Book III, and denounces it as illusory and morally harmful (Chapter 13). In the second, he argues for the immortality of the soul, and completes his argument for justice. Justice is valuable not only in itself but also for its rewards, which come not only in this life but also in the hereafter (Chapter 14).

Guide to Further Reading

For informative and readable accounts of the historical, political and social context of Plato's thought, see A. R. Burn, *The Pelican History of Greece*, A. H. M. Jones, *Athenian Democracy*, A. Andrewes, *Greek Society* respectively. F. M. Cornford, *Before and after Socrates*, gives a brief, excellent and very readable overview of Plato's philosophy in the context of the development of Greek thought. There is an interesting attempt to locate the moral ideas of the *Republic* and Greek ethics more generally in their changing social context in A. MacIntyre, *A Short History of Ethics*, Chapters 1–8.

One of the most helpful and accessible works on the ideas of the *Republic* remains R. L. Nettleship, *Lectures on the* Republic *of Plato*. For greater detail, I. M. Crombie, *An Examination of Plato's Doctrines*, 2 Volumes, is clear and reliable (there is an extended summary of the *Republic* in Volume 1). J. Annas, *An Introduction to Plato's* Republic, is also useful though at times idiosyncratic. R. C. Cross and A. D. Woozley, *Plato's* Republic: *A Philosophical Commentary* is often worth consulting, though the brand of linguistic philosophy which shapes its approach is now very dated. B. Bosanquet, *A Companion to Plato's* Republic and N. P. White's more recent book of the same title give useful help with details of the text.

Works covering the whole range of Plato's thought include G. M. A. Grube, *Plato's Thought*, and A. E. Taylor, *Plato: The Man and His Work*. I include guidance on reading for specific topics at the end of most chapters. Publication details and a selection of further references are given in the Bibliography at the end of the book.

2 The Challenge to Socrates (I.327a – II.367e)

The central issue in the *Republic* is, what is justice? This question is posed in the initial, introductory part, which ends with the challenge to Socrates to defend his view that living justly is good not only for its consequences but also in itself (327a–367e). The remainder of the dialogue consists of Socrates' answer.

Book I (327a–354b), containing the initial discussion of Socrates with Cephalus, Polemarchus and Thrasymachus, has a character strikingly different to that of the rest of the work. In it there is a real dialogue between vividly drawn characters. In the later books, by contrast, Socrates develops his account of justice through what is in effect a monologue. Glaucon and Adeimantus, with whom he is in discussion, hardly ever express contrary views, and do not emerge as distinctive individuals. Book I, moreover, has the standard form of the early Socratic dialogues. Socrates says he 'knows nothing' (354b) about the nature of justice; he does not himself present an account of it. Rather, the other participants do so, and Socrates brings out the inadequacy of their ideas through his critical questioning of them.

For these reasons it has sometimes been suggested that Book I may once have been a separate work, which Plato placed at the beginning of the *Republic* as an introduction. There is no historical evidence to confirm or refute this hypothesis. In any case, there is no discontinuity of theme between Book I and the rest of the work. Quite the contrary. Through these initial encounters Plato leads us with great skill into the main issues of the dialogue.

Cephalus and Polemarchus

The dialogue is realistically set in the Piraeus, the port of Athens. Socrates has walked down there from Athens with Glaucon to make a sacrifice. It takes place in the house of Cephalus and Polemarchus. Through the initial interchanges of Socrates with them and then with Thrasymachus, Glaucon and Adeimantus, we get a good idea of a range of views on justice and morality prevalent at the time.

After some initial scene setting, the discussion soon turns to the topic of justice. Cephalus speaks first. He is an elderly and wealthy merchant who talks with the experience of a long life. He sums up his view in a formula: justice consists in telling the truth and paying one's debts. Socrates challenges this account by asking him whether it would be right to return a knife to a dangerous madman. Cephalus declines to engage in debate with Socrates and hands over the argument to his son, Polemarchus.

Brief as it is, the interchange with Cephalus helps to clarify the nature of the question that is going to be discussed in the dialogue. Socrates rejects Cephalus' attempt to specify the nature of justice by citing examples of particular kinds of just actions, such as telling the truth or repaying debts. These actions are sometimes just, at other times unjust, according to circumstances (331c). What Plato is looking for is an understanding of the defining features that make an action just or unjust. He wants to know about the essential nature of justice, about nature of justice 'in itself' or 'as such'.

Polemarchus now takes up the argument and maintains that justice consists in giving a person his due. He defends this account by quoting the poet Simonides. The poets were the main repository of Greek culture, and it was common practice to cite their words as authority in moral and many other matters, much as religious believers in our culture sometimes cite the Bible. By Plato's time, however, traditional moral ideas were being widely questioned and the interpretation of the poets' words disputed, as Socrates says (332c). The inadequacy of the poets as a source of moral guidance, and the view that philosophical methods should supplant them is an important and controversial theme in the *Republic* as we shall see (Chapter 13).

Cephalus and Polemarchus represent two different kinds of ordinary moral attitude. Both hold certain moral and political views by which they guide their lives, but they have not reflected on them or thought them out critically. In short, they have moral opinions but not a moral philosophy. They are unable to defend their principles when Socrates begins to question them; and, indeed, they are not much concerned to do so. They quickly withdraw, content to leave the argument to others.

Julia Annas maintains that Plato is implicitly criticising Cephalus and Polemarchus for their 'moral complacency'.[1] In the case of Cephalus, at least, that is questionable. He speaks with the wisdom of age and experience and his moderate attitudes in many respects anticipate those of Plato. According to Plato not everyone can or should study philosophy or be able to defend their views philosophically; it is enough if they govern their lives by correct principles, the basis of which they do not fully understand. Philosophy is only for the few.

The charge of complacency is more appropriate in the case of Polemarchus. He is of the younger generation. He confidently cites a maxim from Simonides, but it quickly emerges he has no understanding of it. The demonstration of this is typical of the 'Socratic' method, the first result of which (331d–334b) is the awareness of ignorance and a state of puzzlement (*aporia*). The second stage of the argument with Polemarchus has the more positive purpose of showing that the maxim that justice consists in doing good to friends and harm to enemies is unsatisfactory, since it can never be the aim of morality to cause a person harm (334b–336a).

Much of the argument is framed in terms of an analogy which plays a central role in Greek ethics of this period. The just person is likened to a craftsman with a certain skill, art or craft (*technē*), such as a doctor, shepherd or navigator. What is significant for Plato is that a craftsman has a certain expertise, a knowledge of how to achieve certain results. The doctor knows how to cure disease, the shepherd how to look after the flock.

However, as Plato emphasises in this passage, the analogy must not be pressed too hard. A skill like medicine is a purely neutral sort of knowledge of the means required to achieve a given end. It

---

[1] Annas, *Introduction to Plato's* Republic, p. 21.

can be used either for good or evil, either to cure people or to poison them (333e). This is the sort of skill civil servants are supposed to possess, so that they can carry out government policy, whatever it is. Polemarchus conceives of justice in a similar way. This is implicit in the view that justice is the ability to help one's friends and harm one's enemies. For Plato, however, being just is something quite distinct from the concern with means only and the indifference to ends which characterises the civil service mentality. It is no part of justice to harm people. Justice is not a mere knowledge of means; it is necessarily and essentially aimed at promoting the good.

The Encounter with Thrasymachus

Next, Thrasymachus bursts into the discussion. He is portrayed as a noisy and intemperate extremist. Nevertheless, he introduces a substantial and important philosophy which is then restated and developed, in more moderate terms, by Glaucon and Adeimantus, and which Socrates spends the rest of the dialogue answering.

Thrasymachus is a Sophist. The Sophists were itinerant, paid teachers, who were active in the Greek world at that time. They taught many subjects, but above all oratory and rhetoric, the art of persuasive public speaking, a skill which was useful for political influence in the assembly and law courts. Sophists are the main target of criticism in many of Plato's dialogues. He usually portrays them as caring more for verbal victory than for truth. As a result, the term 'sophistry' has become a synonym for fallacy and error. This is unwarranted. There are important philosophers among the Sophists who put forward theories which are by no means necessarily false or in any simple way fallacious, and which remain influential to this day.

The Sophists were sceptical of conventional moral attitudes and values. Typically, they argued that individual self-interest is the main motivating principle of human life. Their critique was often framed in terms of a distinction which has a central place in Greek thought, between what is due to nature (*phusis*) and what is conventional (*nomos*). Established ideas of morality and justice are human creations, they argued: they are purely man-made and conventional, not natural.

These ideas are evident in Thrasymachus' position. 'Justice', he asserts, is merely the name given to the laws enforced by the ruling powers in a given society, and these laws serve the rulers' own interests. Morality is nothing but 'the interest of the stronger party' (338c), or, to put it in modern jargon, conventional ideas of justice are merely the ideology of the ruling class. People from other classes have no reason to act justly. Indeed, they are foolish to do so. For example, just people dutifully pay their taxes when they are demanded; unjust people avoid paying them if they can and come off better as a result. Absolute tyrants are the happiest of all, for they have the power to flout morality and the law with impunity. The pursuit of self-interest is both natural and right.

Socrates' immediate response to this is framed in terms of an analogy already introduced. He likens the ruler of a state to a craftsman, such as a doctor or a shepherd. Two important implications follow. In the first place, the ruler, just like the doctor and the shepherd, has a certain skill, knowledge or expertise. The view that ruling is a matter of expertise is fundamental to Plato's political philosophy, as will become clear. Second, every craft or skilled activity (*technē*) has a specific purpose or function. The function of a doctor is to care for their patients, the function of the shepherd is to care for the flock. In general, the skill of a craftsman is, or ought to be,[2] exercised for the benefit of its object, and not for the self-interest of the craftsman. Likewise, according to Plato, the aim of government is the good of the governed; this should be the only concern of the true ruler. 'No ruler of any kind, *qua* ruler, exercises his authority ... with his own interest in view ... It is his ... subject's ... interest to which he looks in all he says and does' (342e).

To Thrasymachus, this seems absurdly naive and unrealistic: things are not like this, he insists. The shepherd fattens the sheep for his profit or advantage, not for their good. Rulers act in the same way towards their subjects. Self-interest is the motive principle of human life.[3]

---

[2] Note the ambiguity here, which I will discuss in a moment.

[3] Such views are even more widespread now than in Plato's time. As Adam Smith well puts it, in capitalist society based upon private property, 'it is not from the benevolence of the butcher, the brewer or the baker that we expect our dinner, but from their regard to their own interest. We address ourselves not to their humanity, but to their self-love; and never talk to them of our necessities, but of their advantages' (*Wealth of Nations*, p. 119).

It may well seem that Thrasymachus has the better case here. However, it is important to see that Plato does not deny that people in the position of shepherds, doctors or rulers often act out of self-interest. What he is saying is that they *ought* not to; and, in so far as they act from self-interest, they are not carrying out the essential functions of their crafts. The ruler who acts from self-interest is not acting as a *true* or *proper* ruler should. Thus Plato's idea of a ruler is not purely descriptive of a social role, it embodies an *ideal*.

Plato by no means denies the existence of self-interest in human life (though he does deny that it is the *sole* motivating force). However, throughout the *Republic* he argues that it is a morally harmful and dangerous force. It corrupts individuals and perverts social life. In so far as doctors or teachers are concerned for their fees, to that extent they will be led away from the true purpose of their crafts. This is particularly a danger, Plato believes, with rulers. In his ideal republic, the rulers – the Guardians – are not allowed to own private property or live in families. In this way, Plato hopes to prevent them from benefitting materially from their position or having a personal interest in ruling.

In a confused but important passage, Plato goes on to argue that, though the craftsmen may make money, moneymaking and their specific crafts (herdsmanship, medicine, government, etc.) are quite different activities, which must be sharply distinguished from each other. Plato is mistaken about this. Moneymaking is not a separate activity on a par with medicine or ruling. Doctors who start charging fees are not thereby performing the second and additional activity of 'moneymaking', over and above that of treating patients. Rather, they are performing the same activity, but in different economic conditions – in conditions in which their work has become a commodity. The material content of the work remains the same, but its social and economic form has changed.

In short, Plato is wrong to insist that there are two different *activities* involved when a doctor works for payment. Nevertheless, he has an important point here, for there are two distinguishable *aspects* to the activity. As with all commodities, it has a twofold character: it both meets a need (cures the patient), and exchanges for a fee. Aristotle is the first writer to describe these matters accurately.

Every piece of property has a double use ... one is the proper use of the article in question, the other is not. For example a shoe may be used either to put on your foot or to offer in exchange. Both are uses of the shoe; for even he that gives a shoe to someone who requires a shoe, and receives in exchange coins or food, is making use of the shoe as a shoe, but not the use proper to it, for a shoe is not expressly made for the purposes of exchange. The same is the case with other pieces of property.[4]

In any case, for Plato the proper activity of the doctor is curing the patient; the 'true' doctor, philosopher or ruler does not work for payment. When Plato was writing, Athens was experiencing for the first time the growth of a money economy and the impact of commercial forces. Plato deplores the moral and social impact of these developments, and he opposes and resists them.

The Sophists were a product of these forces and enshrine them in their philosophy. For example, they would teach only for money, and Thrasymachus demands money for his contribution to the discussion, which Glaucon pays (337d). By Plato's standards they are not true philosophers. Likewise, rulers who govern in their own interests are not true rulers. The idea of the 'true' philosopher, doctor or ruler embodies the view that these activities should be performed for the good of their objects – for use and not for profit.

With hindsight, Plato's criticisms of the market may well seem doomed. Like Canute, he was trying to resist the coming tide. However, it would be wrong to dismiss his ideas as of only historical interest on this account. For Plato's views – that the profit motive is hostile to justice and happiness, that society ought not to be based on self-interest, that production should be organised to meet human needs rather than for individual gain – these ideas are, if anything, even more relevant and influential now than when they were first formulated. They remain at the basis of all humanistic and moral criticism of commercial forces and capitalism.

Glaucon and Adeimantus

The encounter with Thrasymachus is only a preliminary skirmish, which sets out some of the ground to be covered. For the results of

---

[4] Aristotle, *Politics* 1257a. Marx describes these two aspects as the object's 'use-value' and 'exchange value', and the two aspects of the work that goes into producing it as 'concrete' and 'abstract' labour (*Capital*, Vol. I, pp. 125–37).

the 'Socratic' methods of argument used in Book I are negative, as Socrates acknowledges when he admits that he still 'knows nothing' about the nature of justice (354b). Though Thrasymachus has been silenced by these methods, his position has not been satisfactorily answered, nor has Plato's own account of justice been explained and defended. Glaucon and Adeimantus express their dissatisfaction at the beginning of Book II. They then restate Thrasymachus' basic outlook in a less belligerent manner and challenge Socrates to refute it.

Glaucon and Adeimantus represent a new attitude towards the question of justice. Unlike Cephalus and Polemarchus, they do not simply accept a traditional view that they are unable to defend; nor are they committed Sceptics, like the Sophist Thrasymachus. They want to believe that there is genuine value in traditional morality, but they are swayed by the Sophists' arguments. They do not know how to defend their convictions against the prevalent scepticism.

With their advent the dialogue takes a less antagonistic and more cooperative form. Plato can now proceed positively and constructively, developing his own philosophy in what is, in effect, a monologue. What this new approach loses by way of dramatic interest, it more than makes up for in terms of results achieved.

Glaucon begins by distinguishing three different ways in which things can be good. They can be either:

1. desirable for their own sake; or
2. desirable both for their own sake and for their consequences; or
3. desirable for their consequences alone.

Justice, says Socrates, is the second and 'highest' kind of good, like wisdom and health. Glaucon would like to agree, but he is beset by doubts. That is not the common view, he says. Most people believe, like Thrasymachus, that acting morally involves self-sacrifice; in itself, it is painful and unpleasant. The only reason to act justly is for the consequences, for the rewards and good reputation that it brings.

Glaucon and Adeimantus spell out this view at length. Glaucon is particularly troubled by the idea that people are naturally self-interested. If we could get away with it, we would ignore the interests of others and satisfy our desires without restraint. To illustrate the point, Glaucon cites the mythical story of Gyges who was said to have found a ring with the magical power to make him invisible. Armed with such a ring, Glaucon suggests, 'there is no one ... who would have such iron strength of will as to do what is right' (360b), for they would be able to steal and do whatever else they wished without any fear of detection.

We do not have this immunity, however. If everyone acted in a purely self-interested way, there would be social chaos and all would suffer. For our own well-being and protection, therefore, we all agree to abide by certain laws and moral principles. What these laws dictate is called 'just' and 'right'. Justice is thus explained in terms of the distinction between what is conventional and what is natural. Rules of justice are not natural. They are conventions to which we agree to adhere only because it is in our interests to do so. Glaucon here gives one of the first formulations of the social contract theory of justice. This theory came to dominate liberal political theory in the seventeenth and eighteenth centuries. Hobbes, Locke, Rousseau, Kant, each put forward versions of it.

According to Glaucon's Hobbesian version, justice is good only for its consequences, not in itself. People obey the principles of morality only under compulsion: 'self-interest [is] the motive which all men naturally follow if they are not forcibly restrained by law and made to respect each other's claims' (359e).

Adeimantus backs up Glaucon's arguments. The most advantageous situation, he maintains, is to have the reputation for justice, while in reality flouting it and pursuing one's own interests. Even in the afterlife we have nothing to fear. He cites the poets Homer and Hesiod to show that the gods themselves can be bought off with gifts and sacrifices. Both Glaucon and Adeimantus then challenge Socrates to defend the view that justice is intrinsically valuable. They ask him to show how the moral life is of value even if it is persecuted, not rewarded, and to demonstrate that justice is good not only for its consequences and external advantages but also in itself.

The remainder of the dialogue constitutes Plato's reply. In the course of it, Plato rejects the views put forward by Thrasymachus, Glaucon and Adeimantus. He questions the pure self-interest theory and develops a fuller and deeper picture of human nature and human happiness. Society is not the result of mere agreement or convention, he maintains, it is a natural order. People do not obey the law only because they are forced. No society could long function in that way. An enduring society must be founded on a large measure of voluntary consent. And acting justly, Plato argues, does indeed lead to true happiness even if it is not rewarded with riches and reputation.

Modern moral theories are usually categorised as either consequentialist or deontological. A consequentialist philosophy, like utilitarianism, maintains that actions or institutions are moral to the extent to which they promote human happiness – it is the consequences of an action which make it moral. Deontologists like Kant, by contrast, insist that matters of justice and right must be sharply distinguished from matters of expediency. Moral principles are categorical, they must be adhered to regardless of the consequences. How does Plato fit into this picture?

Plato maintains that justice is good 'in itself' and not only for its consequences; but it would be a mistake to believe that Plato is giving a deontological account of justice. Summing up their challenge to Socrates, Adeimantus says, 'what we want from you is not only a demonstration that justice is superior to injustice, but a description of the essential effects, harmful or otherwise, which each produces in its possessor' (367a–b). In response, Plato's first concern is to argue that justice is valuable because it leads to the happiness of its possessor, that is, for its consequences. The Kantian idea of moral duties which are obligatory on us categorically and regardless of consequences is foreign to Plato and, indeed, to ancient Greek thought in general.

Despite the language he uses, it is clear that in terms of these modern categories Plato is a consequentialist. When he says that justice is good in itself and not just for its consequences he is distinguishing between different kinds of consequences, internal and external. His claim is that justice carries with it its own reward: it leads to the happiness of its possessor. The just person is the happy person simply because he or she is just, regardless of any external rewards and reputation or harms and evils which may or may not befall them as well. This is the main point Plato is trying to establish throughout the dialogue.

Guide to Further Reading

Helpful accounts of this passage can be found in Nettleship, *Lectures*, Chapters 2–3, and Annas, *Introduction to Plato's* Republic, Chapters 2–3.

There has been an extensive debate about whether the form of Plato's argument is consequentialist. See H. A. Prichard, *Moral Obligation and Duty and Interest*; M. B. Foster, 'A Mistake in Plato's *Republic*'; J. D. Mabbott, 'Is Plato's *Republic* Utilitarian?'; and D. Sachs, 'A Fallacy in Plato's *Republic*'.

3 Basic Principles of Social Life and Human Nature (II.367e–II.376c)

The challenge posed to Socrates concerns the effects of justice on the individual, but Plato begins his response by reminding us that justice is found in societies as well as in individuals. Since justice exists on a 'larger scale' in society and is 'easier to recognize' there (369a), Plato proposes to deal first with the nature of justice in society, and only after that with justice in the individual. He then sketches the features of a rudimentary society in which only the most basic material needs are satisfied. Later, after prompting from Glaucon, he supplements this 'first' society or city (*polis*) with the comforts and refinements of civilisation to construct a 'luxurious' society like the Athens of his time. This brief section lays down the basic principles of social life and human nature which guide Plato's account of his ideal society which follows.

Society and the Individual

Despite the casual way in which it is proposed, the decision to deal with social questions before individual ones is of great philosophical significance; and Plato adheres to this procedure throughout the remainder of the *Republic*. It means that the individual is always considered in a social context. It thus embodies one of the main tenets of Plato's philosophy: that human beings are essentially social creatures.

This conflicts directly with the individualism typically involved in the views of the Sophists, and implied by the social contract theory which Glaucon has just put forward. According to this, human beings are not naturally or necessarily social; social rules are optional conventions, adopted only as a result of mutual agreement and choice. The individual can thus be considered apart from society, and this is the way in which individualist theories describe basic human nature.

In adopting a procedure that always sees the individual in a social context, Plato is implicitly rejecting this individualist approach. He goes on to do so quite explicitly in this section. 'Society originates', he says, 'because the individual is not self-sufficient, but has many needs which he cannot supply himself' (369b). Although this observation is cast in a historical form, it is clear that Plato's real purpose is analytical. He is not concerned to trace the genesis of society, but rather to describe the essential features of, and necessary conditions for, social life. His point would be better put by saying that individuals are and always have been social. We are not and never have been self-sufficient; we depend on others for the satisfaction of even our basic material needs. Social life – social interdependence and cooperation – is not conventional and optional, it is a natural and necessary feature of human life.

Aristotle shares this view. Even more clearly than Plato he insists that 'man is a social animal'.[1] The individualist view is that the individual is logically prior to society, in that there cannot be a society without individuals whereas an individual can exist without a society. Aristotle rejects this. The human individual, he argues, cannot in fact exist without society. This is what he means by the paradoxical seeming dictum that 'society is prior to the individual'.[2] Like Plato he believes that the individual is not self-sufficient. This is not to deny that an individual human being could survive entirely on its own without any contact whatever with others from birth onwards.[3] In the complete absence of socialisation, however, it would be a human being 'only in name', as Aristotle puts it. It would be a mere member of the biological species *homo sapiens*, without any distinctively human moral or psychological characteristics.

[1] Aristotle, *Ethics* 1097b.
[2] Aristotle, *Politics* 1253a.
[3] A hermit or a Robinson Crusoe, who has been brought up in society but subsequently isolated from it, has been socially formed and is excluded here.

The Organic Analogy

Notoriously, Margaret Thatcher said that 'there is no such thing as society, only individuals pursuing their own interests'. Plato's account of the relation of the individual to society is the direct opposite of this. It is worked out in terms of an analogy, which plays a central role in his social thought, between society and a living organism such as the human body.

A living body is not a mere collection of independent parts: brain, heart, limbs and so on. It is a an organic entity, a living whole. It is a unified system, a structured whole, in which each part has its own function to perform within the context of the whole, as an organ of the organism. So, too, a society is not a mere collection of isolated individuals each independently pursuing their own separate interests. It is a structured and unified whole, in which the individuals who compose it, as its members, have specific roles and functions as members of the community, as parts of the whole.

Two consequences follow from this. First, a society, like an organism, is not simply the sum of its parts considered as separate and isolated units; it is those parts, unified and organised into a structured whole. There are properties of the whole which are not reducible to the properties of the parts. Moreover, the interest of the organism as a whole is not simply a matter of the interests of all its parts taken separately. Similarly, a community has an interest of its own which is not reducible to the sum of the interests of the individuals that comprise it. This notion of the social interest, as something distinct from the mere aggregate of separate individual interests, is a key term in Plato's social and political thought.

Second, just as a part of the body is an organ of an organism, so the individual is essentially a social being, a member of the community, a part of a larger whole. The interests of the individual must be understood in this context. The individual can achieve satisfaction and happiness only in society, by carrying out a specific role as a member of the community, for individuals are not self-sufficient: they can function and flourish only as parts of the whole.

In normal conditions, the different parts of the body work harmoniously together as the organs of a single organism. There is no inevitable conflict between the different organs of the body, or between the organs and the body as a whole. Such conflicts arise only in conditions of illness. So, too, according to Plato, there is no necessary conflict of interests between the individuals in a society or between the individual and society as a whole. Such conflicts are a sign that the society is malfunctioning. In these conditions the individual also suffers. But if each individual fulfils their function as a member of the community, harmony is possible; and, in such circumstances, the individual will thrive and flourish too.

According to some critics the organic analogy involves the view that society is some mysterious additional entity 'over and above' the individuals composing it.[4] There is no suggestion of this in Plato. Plato does, however, reject the extreme individualist position. Society is not simply a collection of separate individuals. It is a totality, a community, of which the constituent individuals are members, and in which they are related together and unified *as a whole*. In that sense, there is such a thing as society which is something 'more' than the mere aggregate of separate individuals who make it up. But this is not to say that it is some further entity, distinct from them, for the 'more' here resides in the structure of their mutual relationships.

As I have just stressed, Plato also maintains that the social interest is something 'over and above' the sum of purely individual interests; and, as we shall see, the interests of particular individuals can come into conflict with it. In this case, however, it is the individual's interest as a member of the community which conflicts with their interest as a mere isolated individual. Again, there is no suggestion that the social interest is some additional entity, separate and distinct from the interests of individuals. Quite the contrary, the social interest is the totality of the interests that individuals have as members of the community, as parts of the whole.[5]

Specialisation and the Division of Labour

These views are still influential. They continue to provide the basis for the main alternative to individualist social philosophy. In so

---

[4] Annas, *Introduction to Plato's* Republic, pp. 179–80. On this basis it is sometimes argued that the organic analogy has sinister totalitarian political implications. I will come back to this issue in Ch. 6 below.

[5] Similar issues are raised by Rousseau's notion of the 'general will' and its relation to the particular will of the individual, *The Social Contract*, I. vii.

far as this is so, however, they must be distinguished from another set of ideas in Plato, which run directly counter to most modern social thought: the belief in a natural social hierarchy based upon natural human differences.

If the organic analogy is pursued beyond the point to which I have so far taken it, it may well lead in this direction, and this is the direction in which Plato takes it. Just as the different organs of the body have different characteristics which fit them for different functions so, too, different individuals have different natural abilities which fit them for different occupations and social roles. 'No two of us are born exactly alike. We have different aptitudes, which fit us for different jobs' (370a–b).[6]

Plato first introduces this principle to justify a basic economic division of labour, but he soon goes on to apply it to social and political arrangements more generally. He begins by suggesting that production is more efficient if it is organised cooperatively, so that different workers specialise in the particular trades – farming, building, weaving, etc. – for which they are naturally suited, rather than each trying to be self-sufficient and produce everything that they need for themselves.

Plato's arguments for the division of labour are often compared with those of later economists like Adam Smith. There are fundamental differences, however. Plato's essential point is that there are innate differences between people, which provide a natural basis for specialisation. Smith is sceptical of this whole set of ideas.

> The difference of natural talents in different men is, in reality, much less than we are aware of, and the very different genius which appears to distinguish men of different professions, when grown up to maturity, is not upon many occasions so much the cause as the effect of the division of labour. The difference between the most dissimilar characters, between a philosopher and a common street porter, for example, seems to arise not so much from nature as from habit, custom and education.[7]

Smith defends the division of labour only as a more economically efficient way of organising production. For Plato, by contrast, the

---

[6] This idea is expressed by Menenius Agrippa in the fable of the belly in Shakespeare, *Coriolanus*, I, i.
[7] Smith, *Wealth of Nations*, p. 120.

division of labour is not just an economic matter. Specialisation is a fundamental moral and social principle which governs the entire construction of his ideal society.

These wider implications emerge as soon as we move beyond the economic realm that Plato first considers. For Plato begins by considering a society which caters only for the most basic necessities of life: for plain and simple food, shelter and clothing. Glaucon, however, objects. A society like this would be austere in the extreme. It would allow only an animal level of existence; it would be no better than a 'community of pigs' (372d). People have further desires which develop and multiply as society grows. They will not be content with such primitive conditions, they want the comforts and refinements of civilisation. Reluctantly, Socrates agrees to consider a 'luxurious' society in which these appetites and desires are also catered for.

In the first, rudimentary society, only a few basic occupations are required. With the growth of civilisation and the desire for comforts and luxuries, new occupations are needed to provide them. Thus society embarks on a process of material and social development without any inherent limits (373d). In time, it inevitably seeks to expand its territory, and thus it comes into conflict with other similar societies. The result is war. The society now requires soldiers to defend it. In accordance with the principle of specialisation, Plato argues that these should be a separate professional group, a class of 'Guardians', naturally fitted by their particular qualities of temperament for the role. In the fifth century, professional soldiers had become the norm in Greece, so there would have been nothing surprising to Plato's contemporaries in this suggestion.

Not only does a new social group develop with the growth of the luxurious society, but new aspects of human nature emerge as well. This becomes clear when Plato turns to consider the qualities needed in the Guardians. They should be like watchdogs, he maintains, combining fierceness and courage in the face of the enemy with gentleness towards friends. The fierceness is characteristic of spirit (*thūmos*) which, as we shall later see, is regarded by Plato as one of the three basic parts of the self or soul (*psuchē*). Spirit is shown in aggression, ambition and also in a sense of honour. In the Guardians this needs to be kept in control by the philosophical or rational part of the self, which draws us to that which is familiar to us or akin to us. This may be felt as friendship towards fellow citizens, but it may also be manifest as an attraction towards things which are beautiful or true. For, according to Plato, in our love of such things the rational part of the self recognises what is akin to it in the objective world.[8]

Later, Plato divides the Guardians into two distinct groups: the Rulers of the society in whom reason predominates, and the 'Auxiliaries' or soldiers, who are governed by spirit (412c–413d). These two groups, together with the Productive Workers, according to Plato, constitute the three basic classes which perform the three basic functions in society. However, from this point on, the Workers drop out of the picture almost entirely. Plato's whole attention now turns to the Guardians and their training.

The Social Order

For Plato, ruling is a craft which, as we have seen, he conceives by analogy with activities like medicine or navigation. It involves skill and expertise. Only those who have acquired this skill should be rulers. This skill, according to Plato, lies in philosophy, the ultimate purpose of which is to give knowledge of 'the Form of the Good'. This is the ultimate value, ideal or end which should guide society in all its actions. It is not a matter of mere subjective opinion; it can be objectively known. Only those who have acquired this knowledge should be rulers.[9]

Moreover, Plato believes, only some have the natural abilities to acquire it. According to the principle of the natural division of labour, these people – and only these people – should be rulers of the state; and they should specialise in ruling, they should have no other occupation. Likewise, the military work of the Auxiliaries involves particular skills, and only those who are naturally endowed with them should be Auxiliaries. Those with natural abilities for productive work should be Workers, though Plato spends little time discussing these abilities. Often he appears to assume that there are no special skills involved in being a Productive Worker. This is

---

[8] See Ch. 6 below for a fuller account of the parts of the self.
[9] See Ch. 9 below.

characteristic of Plato's philosophy; his whole interest is focused on the Guardians, on the Rulers and Auxiliaries. In common with many other political thinkers before the modern era, his work is addressed entirely to the rulers of society and his concern is to determine the conditions which will produce good rulers.

In this way Plato argues that society must be divided into three distinct classes or orders. This structure is rigidly hierarchical, and the fundamental division in it is between the rulers and the ruled. A few are born to rule, the majority to be ruled. For most people, Plato believes, are incapable of leading an autonomous life; they are better off if they are paternalistically governed, like children by wiser parents. 'In our state', as he bluntly puts it, 'the desires of the less reputable majority are controlled by the desires and wisdom of the superior minority' (431c–d). This arrangement, he believes, is naturally ordained and essential for the well-being of society. These ideas are expressed in the 'foundation myth', the 'myth of origins', according to which all members of the community are brothers and sisters, 'born of the same mother earth'; but when God fashioned them, he added gold to those who are qualified to be Rulers, silver to the Auxiliaries, and iron and bronze to the Workers (415a–c).

All this is quite alien to modern thinking, but it would not have been so to Plato's contemporaries. Athens was a society based on slavery and imbued with the idea of natural inequalities.[10] Similar inequalitarian ideas recur throughout ancient and medieval social thought. They are evident in the medieval view that the feudal class structure constituted a divinely ordained order. More than a few traces of this attitude linger on in British life to this day. It is given familiar expression in the nineteenth-century hymn,

> All things bright and beautiful,
> All creatures great and small,
> All things wise and wonderful,
> The Lord God made them all.

---

[10] The widespread acceptance of the idea of natural hierarchy is perhaps indicated by the fact that Plato does not seek to justify it in philosophical terms, but presents it in the form of a myth. Aristotle, by contrast, attempts to give a theoretical justification of the idea of natural inequality (*Politics* I.iii–vii, xii–xiii).

> The rich man in his castle,
> The poor man at his gate,
> God made them, high or lowly,
> And ordered their estate.

However, there is also an important difference between the feudal view and Plato's which should be noted. The feudal class system was hereditary, whereas Plato's ideal republic is supposed to be a strict meritocracy. Following the logic of his principle of the division of labour, social roles are determined purely on the basis of ability. As the 'foundation myth' states, although children often have the same abilities as their parents, this is not invariably so. One of the tasks of the educational system is to select people according to ability, even though it is not clear how this is supposed to work in practice.[11] Nevertheless, as with the feudal outlook, Plato assumes that there are inborn differences of individual ability which provide the basis for a natural social hierarchy and political order. These ideas are now almost universally rejected. For although there are, no doubt, considerable natural differences of ability, they do not justify the right to rule, as Plato maintains. The notion of a natural hierarchy has passed away along with the social system which it describes and legitimates.

Needs and Desires

As we have seen, Plato begins his reply by considering the simplest sort of society, in which only basic needs are met. But Glaucon objects. Reluctantly, Plato agrees to consider a 'luxurious' society in which desires beyond the survival minimum are also catered for. The reasons for his reluctance are important; they introduce a theme which runs right through the *Republic* and which is fundamental to Plato's social and moral thought.

According to Plato, our only true needs are for the basic necessities of life. These are the 'necessary desires', the satisfaction of which is all we need for a happy life and a happy society. Desires beyond them are for non-necessities, for luxuries. These are what Plato calls 'unnecessary' desires; more recently they have been

---

[11] Aristotle criticises Plato's proposals in these terms, *Politics* 1262b.

termed 'false' needs.[12] Such desires may seem just as pressing and urgent as the necessary desires, but for Plato the criterion of their necessity is not their subjectively felt strength. These desires are unnecessary, he maintains, first because we can survive without their being satisfied, and second because their satisfaction does not lead to happiness, either for the individual or society (558d–559a). The social proliferation of superfluous desires and luxuries to satisfy them leads to what Plato, using the organic analogy, calls a 'sick' and 'inflamed' society (372e).

The corrupting and divisive influence of excessive wealth is one of the major themes of Plato's philosophy. His ideal is a society of spartan simplicity. In view of this, commentators have been puzzled as to why he agrees to move beyond the simple society he describes first and consider a luxurious state, which he then has to purge of its luxury. His whole philosophy seems to point to the conclusion that we would be happier in the first, simple society. Yet, if we accept this conclusion, the purpose of the rest of the book becomes a mystery, since it focuses exclusively on developed, 'luxurious' forms of society.

Plato gives no clear answer to this question. We can only speculate. The move to a luxurious society is of great significance. It not only introduces superfluous material goods; it also leads to the emergence of the Guardians as a separate group. They are not just another occupational group, a further branch of the economic division of labour on a par with the shepherds, carpenters, etc. of the first society. They are a quite different kind of group: they have a political and not simply an economic role.

This indicates an important difference between the first society and the luxurious society which replaces it. The first society is a purely economic arrangement, held together by the forces of mutual economic dependence. It has no government authority to maintain its unity. In this respect, it is like those natural forms of social arrangement that are found among social animals such as ants or bees. The luxurious society is a quite different sort of organisation. It is governed by rulers whose conscious task it is to preserve the society both from external threat and internal disruption. It is divided into rulers and ruled. It is guided by notions

---

[12] H. Marcuse, *One Dimensional Man*, pp. 4–6.

of justice and injustice. It is not only an economic and social organisation but also a political one.

If the first society is, indeed, Plato's ideal, then the advent of luxurious conditions constitutes a veritable Fall into political division. However, this Fall from the natural harmony of some prehistoric Eden is the path of development that all existing societies have in fact taken. For Plato to have confined his discussion to the situation before the Fall would have been for him to ignore actual social reality. It may seem that this is something that Plato is quite willing to do. He is often accused of being a utopian dreamer who turns his back on the real world, and fixes his gaze on the ideal. He even presents his own approach in this way. Nevertheless this is a misrepresentation of Plato's work which cannot do justice to its contemporary political focus. The *Republic* is not a mere utopia. It is clearly intended as a critique of the Athens of its time. As Hegel says, 'Plato's *Republic*, which passes proverbially as an empty ideal, is in essence nothing but an interpretation of the nature of Greek ethical life'.[13]

If this is correct, Plato's ideas are not empty and unreal, they are related to the prevailing conditions of social and political life. Perhaps this is why he keeps his attention on conditions after the Fall. For in reality, we live after the Fall; we have left behind the state of natural and primitive simplicity, and can never go back. What were once, perhaps, luxuries are now necessities; we live in a political world of justice and injustice, of rulers and ruled. This is our situation, these are the problems we face; and philosophy, as Plato realises, must address itself to them if it is to be of any relevance or use.

Guide to Further Reading

M. B. Foster, *The Political Philosophies of Plato and Hegel*, Chapters 1–2, and Cross and Woozley, *Plato's* Republic, Chapters 4–5, are particularly useful on this section. Also worth consulting are Nettleship, *Lectures*, Chapter 4, and Barker, *Political Thought of*

---

[13] G. W. F. Hegel, *The Philosophy of Right*, p. 10. Cf. Barker's view that the *Republic* 'is a practical treatise ... written in reaction against political conditions, and, in its attempt at reconstruction, based upon contemporary facts' (*The Political Thought of Plato and Aristotle*, p. 160).

Plato and Aristotle, Chapter 3 Section 4. See also J. Neu, 'Plato's Analogy of State and Individual'. For individualist criticism of Plato's approach of the kind I will be discussing more fully below, see Popper, *The Open Society*, Volume I, Chapter 10.

4 Education and the Life of the Guardians (II.376c–IV.427e)

On the basis of the principles discussed in the last chapter, Plato now begins to construct his ideal society. Few will find it attractive, let alone ideal. In accordance with the principle of the natural division of labour, it is rigidly divided into the three classes or orders of Rulers, Auxiliaries and Productive Workers. Membership of these classes is determined strictly by ability, both for women and men. The Guardians are the rulers. The first stage of their education is the main topic of the present section. This is common to both Auxiliaries and Rulers. It lasts until about the age of 18, and is followed by two years of military training. At this point, the future Rulers are chosen after a careful selection process and given a lengthy higher education (described in Book VII).

The Guardians have absolute power over every aspect of life. Plato is particularly concerned that they exercise this power in a benevolent way like 'true' rulers, not to further their own interests but for the social interest. The specific arrangements for the lives of the Guardians which he outlines are all designed to ensure this, both negatively and positively.

The negative measures which Plato proposes to prevent the development of self-interest are sweeping. The Rulers live a life which has been well described as a sort of 'military monasticism'.[1] They are not permitted to have personal property or to accumulate wealth. They are required to live and eat communally, in a plain and simple manner, 'like soldiers in a camp' (416e). The family is abolished. Children are reared in public nurseries. Sexual relations

---

[1] Nettleship, *Lectures*, p. 136.

are strictly planned and controlled to limit the population and regulate breeding according to eugenic principles. In all these matters, women are treated equally with men. These proposals do not apply to the Workers, only to the Rulers and Auxiliaries. They are briefly described at the end of the present section (412b–427e) and Plato returns to them later. I shall postpone discussion of them until Chapter 8.

Education is the main positive means of instilling knowledge of the social interest and a sense of social cooperation and purpose. It is also the mechanism through which future Rulers are selected. The present section is mainly devoted to a lengthy account of the first stage of the education of the Guardians.

The Social and Moral Role of Education

Plato attaches enormous importance to education. His reasons for this are easily misunderstood. He is accused of proposing a system of mass indoctrination, designed to brainwash the people into docile acceptance of the Guardians' will. In fact, Plato is remarkably unconcerned about the mass of the people. It is doubtful whether the education he describes in the *Republic* is intended for them at all. He takes their obedience and acquiescence almost entirely for granted. The main fault with Plato's educational system is rather its elitism; it is designed purely as a training for the Rulers.

In the ideal society, Plato believes, formal legislation is minimal. There is no framework of individual rights, and no mention even of a constitution. Plato relies on education to fulfil many of the functions which these political mechanisms perform in the modern state. It carries the main responsibility for ensuring that the state is orderly and well ruled. It has two main tasks.

It provides the mechanism for selecting the Rulers. For the Guardians are not elected, nor are they a hereditary aristocracy or caste. They qualify purely on the basis of ability; and it is the job of the educational system to identify and select those who have the requisite abilities for ruling positions. Although Plato believes that the abilities required by the Guardians are inborn and innate, education is needed in order to develop and realise them. This is the second and most important function of education. Since there are no constitutional or legal constraints on the activities of the Guardians, their selection and education are the sole means of ensuring that they will be good rulers.

Moreover, Plato maintains, in a well-ordered society, people will be obedient to authority primarily because of their upbringing and education, not because they are coerced by the threat of punishment. This is a central theme of Plato's social thought and an important point of contrast with the individualist philosophy of the Sophists. For their view, as we have seen, is that human beings are essentially self-interested and in conflict with each other. Social cooperation is not natural; it is possible only as a compromise, under the constraining force of the law and the threat of punishment.

Plato, by contrast, argues that there is no necessary or inevitable conflict between individuals, or between the individual and society. With the appropriate upbringing and social conditions, and with good will, it is possible for people to live together cooperatively without the threat of force. This is the ideal that Plato envisages. Whether this ideal is genuinely possible is one of the main issues posed by the *Republic*. Plato himself is very aware of the great problems there are in creating and sustaining such a cooperative community. It is in this context that his educational proposals must be seen. In a later work, the *Laws*, he seems to have had doubts about the practicality of such a society; for in that work, he concentrates on a 'second-best' state governed by law. In the *Republic*, however, his main purpose is to describe and defend this ideal, particularly against the individualist outlook of the Sophists.

For Plato, the main purpose of education is moral and social rather than academic. Its aim is not primarily to impart any specific body of knowledge or set of skills, but rather to develop the character and abilities required in the Guardians. Although Plato believes that these abilities are innate, they develop only as a result of education. Plato's general views about education are most graphically expressed in the allegory of the cave in Book VII. There Plato likens the process of education to getting the eyes – which the self already possesses – to turn towards the light. 'We must reject the conception of education professed by those who say that they can put into the mind knowledge that was not there before – rather as if they could put sight into blind eyes' (518c). With this metaphor Plato suggests that education is not a matter of imparting new information or inculcating new skills. Rather, it involves developing and bringing out powers which are already latent in the self. These are the powers to apprehend beauty, truth and goodness – the powers of reason, which are also at the basis of human cooperation.

These powers will be encouraged to develop, Plato believes, if the self is surrounded by beauty, truth and goodness from its earliest years. The main job of education is to create an environment of this sort. Then harmony and order will penetrate into the infant self 'and take a most powerful hold' imparting to it 'beauty and grace'. In the process, the developing individual will come to love beauty and shun ugliness, 'even when he is still young and cannot understand the reason for so doing'. And when he is an adult and his reason has developed and he perceives something beautiful, 'he will recognize and welcome her as a familiar friend' (402a–b).

The Content and Form of Education

Plato's general account of the process of education, both in this section and in Book VII, contains some of the most inspiring and enthralling passages in the whole dialogue. But this general account contrasts sharply with the specific and detailed proposals which occupy the bulk of this section. These seem authoritarian and constricting in the extreme.

Plato's plans are based on existing Greek practice, reformed as Plato thinks necessary to purge society of luxury and excess. In Athens, education – which was for boys only – took place in privately run schools, and was the responsibility of the family. Plato adopts the Spartan model in making education the responsibility of the state and, in view of Plato's ideas about the role of women, we must suppose that he extends it to girls, though there is no mention of this in this section.

As regards the contents of education he keeps to the pattern which was traditional in Athens (376e).[2] After a basic training in reading and writing, education was divided into two branches:

---

[2] A standard Greek education along similar lines is outlined by Protagoras in *Protagoras* 325d–326e.

physical training (*gymnastikē*) and education in the arts (*mousikē*). The latter encompassed all the activities over which the Muses preside, and included not only music but all the arts, philosophy and even such subjects as arithmetic and geometry as well.

Plato says very little about physical education. The section devoted to it is largely taken up with a polemic against doctors and lawyers (403c–412a). Physical training, Plato argues, should not aim to strengthen only the body: it also has a moral purpose. It develops the spirited side of the self. This needs to be balanced by the rational part, developed by training in the arts, in order to produce a harmonious character, which is the ultimate aim of both branches of education (410e–412a).

Plato has a great deal to say about education in the arts. He focuses particularly on poetry, which occupied a central place in ancient Greek education and culture. A major part of a child's education consisted of learning and reciting the poets, particularly Homer and Hesiod. Their works were thought to embody the society's accumulated moral wisdom and many of its religious ideas. They were frequently cited as authorities in argument, in the way that Polemarchus does at the beginning of the dialogue.

Furthermore, the works of the poets were recited aloud rather than read silently to oneself, and they were often sung to the accompaniment of the lyre. Hence Plato's elaborate discussion of the effects of 'imitation' (*mimēsis*) when the reader takes the part of different characters (392c–400c). Although some of Plato's concerns in this section are now of interest only to students of ancient Greek culture, he also raises a number of general issues which are still fundamental.

The young child is particularly impressionable. The literature and music it first encounters, even the stories it is first told, have a major impact on its subsequent development. Plato plans to subject all these to the closest political control and strictly censor anything judged false, harmful or demoralising. Plato is particularly concerned that they should convey true ideas about the gods, and that they should have a beneficial and not harmful effect on character.

To the modern reader, Plato's readiness to 'correct' – to bowdlerise and censor – Homer and Hesiod and the other poets is alarming. As regards the contents of their work, Plato proposes to censor all passages which portray the gods in what he regards as a false light, as causing harm or engaging in deception or even changing their form (which the Greek gods do frequently), for god, according to Plato, is good and true and unchanging. Furthermore, the semi-divine heroes of Greek legend should always be portrayed as admirable models to emulate. Any suggestion that they can behave in a cowardly or intemperate manner must be removed.

Plato goes on to give lengthy consideration to the form or style of the arts, particularly music. The details of his discussion do not concern us here. However, we must not lose sight of the general point that Plato is making: namely, that the arts have important moral effects and their role in education should be assessed in moral terms. The art and music to which children are exposed in their upbringing should portray things truthfully and be beneficial and not harmful to the development of their character.

Censorship in Education

Plato's educational ideas have attracted a huge amount of discussion and criticism. As regards his overall approach, Plato is often treated as the archetypal enemy of the liberal social values usually associated with classical Athenian society. He is accused of wanting to drag Athens back to an earlier form of 'closed' tribal society, by brainwashing its citizens and suppressing all criticism and dissent.[3]

This interpretation is untenable. Plato is indeed a conservative thinker, but not of this archaic kind. He is not suggesting that people should have a simple and unquestioning faith in traditional institutions. Even if he had wanted this, he was well aware that by the time he was writing any possibility of it had long past. The questioning and criticism of traditional beliefs which characterised the Greek enlightenment was widespread. Plato himself was a product of this period.[4] Rationalism – belief in the power of reason – is central to his philosophy. It is reason, not blind faith, to which he always appeals as the source of practical guidance and the means of settling disputes. This is what makes Plato, despite his conservatism, still seem such a modern thinker.

---

[3] This is one of the main themes of Popper, *The Open Society*, Vol. I.
[4] E. R. Dodds, *The Greeks and the Irrational*, Chs 6–7.

Nevertheless, many modern readers are horrified by Plato's willingness to control and even censor the arts. At least where young children are concerned, however, modern educational practice is not so very different. Few people would argue for pure *laissez-faire* in matters of elementary education. It is almost universally agreed that the educator should exercise careful control over the materials made available to young children. And many would agree with Plato's reasons: the young are impressionable and it is the job of the teacher to encourage the appreciation of beauty, truth and goodness, and to benefit not harm the developing child. Material that is judged to be false or harmful should be excluded.

In making such judgements, Plato is criticised for assuming his own 'infallibility'.[5] He is accused of making the unwarranted assumption that, as teacher, he always knows best what is true or false, good or evil. It is true that Plato believes that there are objective truths and objective values which can be known with certainty; but those views are simply not involved here. All education involves decisions about the curriculum and the selection of material. And in the process, every teacher must commit themselves to some view of what is true and good, and control the inclusion or exclusion of material in the light of it. Initially at least, all teachers do inevitably act as if they know best, or at least better than their pupils – this is not peculiar to Plato.

However, there are other and more telling criticisms. Plato's ultimate aim is to produce a group of rational and critical Guardians who will, like Socrates, be prepared to follow the logic of their ideas without fear or favour – to go wherever 'the wind of the argument' carries them (394d). Children have not yet developed these powers of rational judgement; the aim of Plato's educational system is to develop them. Plato's educational methods, it is argued, are not well designed for this purpose. It is difficult to see how Plato's authoritarian and restricted regime can hope to have the desired effect. If people are to develop the ability for critical reasoning it would seem that they must have some experience of it, but this opportunity is rigorously excluded, at least in the first stage of Plato's education (which lasts up to the age of eighteen).

[5] J. S. Mill, *On Liberty*, p. 143.

This line of thought is eloquently expressed by John Stuart Mill. People must be allowed to question and to err if they are to reach a genuine understanding of the truth, rather than learning doctrines by rote and holding them as lifeless and meaningless dogmas. Unless even true opinion is 'vigorously and earnestly contested', Mill argues, 'it will ... be held in the manner of a prejudice, with little comprehension or feeling of its rational grounds ... The meaning of the doctrine itself will be in danger of being lost, or enfeebled, and deprived of its vital effect'.[6] In other words, there is a value in critical and opposing views even when they are mistaken. As Mill observes, it is ironical that Plato fails to recognise this, since his own Socratic dialogues are the first, and still the best and most celebrated, examples of this critical method in practice.[7]

Indoctrination and Education

To present-day readers, Plato's idea of surrounding the growing child with what he regards as examples of beauty, truth and goodness may look like an attempt at conditioning and indoctrination. According to the conditioning view of education, human nature is a blank and neutral material like clay which is moulded and formed by influences from outside. It is important to see that Plato has a very different idea of the educational process. As we have seen, he rejects the view that education is like putting sight into blind eyes: it does not involve imposing something new on a blank self from outside. It can only bring out (or stifle) powers which are already latent in the self. And it can do this only when the order of the surrounding environment is consonant with the inner and still latent powers of reason in the self.

Another image that Plato uses for the educational process is of a plant which flourishes in the right conditions but withers in adverse ones (491d). His plan is to surround the child with beauty, truth and goodness in order to promote the growth of these qualities in its developing self. His censorship of poetry and the arts is aimed at that end. Laudable as these aims are, there is a

[6] Mill, *On Liberty*, pp. 180–1.
[7] Ibid., pp. 171–2.

danger that the education he proposes will end up having the opposite effect. In reality, the world is not always beautiful, it is often ugly; and people are not always virtuous, they are often cowardly, intemperate and unjust. Those on the receiving end of Plato's education will get censored, distorted and ultimately quite false picture of the world. Their education will be a poor preparation for the world as it actually is. To learn about this, they will have to go out of class, 'behind the bike sheds' as it were. Surely there are better ways of organising education than this.

This raises a familiar dilemma for the teacher. The aim of education is to develop the good qualities in young people, but they are growing up in a world full of evils. Should they be protected from them, or should they be taught about them and hence exposed to them? Plato is well aware of this issue. He explicitly takes the side of protection. Whereas the doctor's training should include some first-hand experience of being ill, he argues, moral education does not require that we ourselves should have experience of wrongdoing (408d–409e).

> The mind must not be brought up from its youth to associate with wickedness, or to run through a whole range of crimes in order to get first-hand experience on which to be able to judge them quickly in other people, as the doctor does with diseases of the body: on the contrary, the mind must, while it is still young, remain quite without experience of or contact with bad characters, if its condition is to be truly good and its judgements just. That is why people of good character seem simple when they are young, and are easily taken in by dishonesty – because they have nothing corresponding in themselves to give them a sympathetic understanding of wickedness.[8]

Of course, children must be protected and sheltered from much of the wickedness and evil of the world, particularly when they are young. At the same time, however, it is the task of education to introduce the growing child to the realities of the world. Plato's educational programme makes little provision for this.

In this connection, an important role that literature and the arts play in education is, arguably, to give insight into a diversity of new perspectives and unfamiliar worlds, to open up access to a variety of different characters and situations, both good and evil. But Plato

---

[8] *Republic* 409a.

sees no benefit in this. Quite the contrary. In education he wants to restrict experience not widen it out. Literature and art involve a process of imitation and identification (*mimēsis*). By imaginatively identifying with different characters we take on different roles.[9] According to Plato, this will be harmful to the Guardians if these roles are those of disreputable characters (396c), or of women or slaves (395d–e). The Guardians should be allowed to identify only with people of good character and of their own sex and social class.

Plato justifies this view by appealing to the principle of specialisation in the division of labour (394e). At first this principle seems out of place in this context. But just as the Guardians and the other classes are supposed to have specific natural abilities which fit them for a particular specialised function to which they should confine themselves, so too their education and perspective is to be specialised and restricted.

The modern reader is likely to object that a wide range of identifications will make us more understanding and sympathetic towards the experience and activities of others. But Plato is not interested in this. The notion that people can benefit from understanding a diversity of viewpoints is a distinctively modern idea, presupposing a universalistic and equalitarian conception of human nature. It is quite foreign to Plato's philosophy, which is founded upon the idea that we each have specific natures which assign us to fixed and different 'places' in a natural hierarchy.

Propaganda and Truth

One aspect of Plato's philosophy which attracts much criticism is its apparent disregard for the value of truthfulness. According to Popper, for example, 'nothing is more in keeping with Plato's totalitarian morality than his advocacy of propaganda lies'.[10] What Popper is referring to is the fact that in certain cases Plato quite explicitly recommends lying by the Guardians. There are two prominent examples in the *Republic*.

---

[9] It should be remembered that Plato is talking about the representation of these roles involved in dramatic recitation, which involves imitating and actually taking the part of these characters. Nevertheless, similar issues arise with the imaginative identifications involved in being a mere spectator at a performance or reading silently to oneself.

[10] *The Open Society*, Vol. I, p. 141.

The first is the 'foundation myth', the story of their origins to be inculcated into all members of the community. According to this, they are all 'brothers of the same mother earth' (and sisters presumably), but when they were created, gold was included in those qualified to be Rulers, silver in the Auxiliaries and iron and bronze in the Workers. Children will usually, though not invariably, resemble their parents. 'The first and most important of god's commandments to the Rulers is that in the exercise of their function as Guardians their principal care must be to watch the mixture of metals in the characters of their children' in order to ensure that each is assigned to its proper class. 'This they must do because there is a prophecy that the State will be ruined when it has Guardians of silver or bronze' (415b–c).

This story is explicitly described as a fable, a fiction, a falsehood: Plato calls it a 'magnificent myth' (414b). This phrase is otherwise translated as 'noble lie' or 'noble falsehood'. 'Myth', 'lie' and 'falsehood' here are translations of the Greek *pseudos*. This word does not carry the implication of a deliberate intention to deceive involved in the concept of lying. Indeed, the foundation myth is not a piece of cynical propaganda used by the Rulers to persuade the people to accept their lot, as writers like Popper suggest. In the first place, it is not aimed only at the common people. On the contrary, it is intended initially for the Rulers and Auxiliaries (414d), though Plato hopes that in time all the citizens will come to believe it (415d). Moreover, there is an important sense in which it is not a lie, not even a falsehood, at all. Plato genuinely believes that there are these three types of individual. For him, therefore, the story expresses the truth, although in mythical form.[11]

Nevertheless, Plato does quite explicitly advocate lying when it is necessary for the social interest. 'It will be for the rulers of our city ... if anyone, to deceive citizen or enemy for the good of the State; no one else must do so' (389b). The clearest example of straightforward deception is the rigging of the lots which control mating (459c–460b). However, even this is not the unscrupulous manipulation denounced by critics. It is an integral part of a larger, well-considered and defensible philosophical position.

---

[11] Plato often uses stories and myths to express philosophical ideas in his writings, even though in Book X he appears to condemn them as incapable of expressing knowledge. For further discussion see Ch. 13 below.

For Plato, the values of goodness and truth are not generally in conflict: it is wrong to suggest that he advocates widespread use of false propaganda. In the rare cases in which a conflict does arise, considerations of what is for the good must ultimately take precedence and prevail over regard for the truth. This is a tenable view, though it raises difficult issues of political morality. Thus, it can be argued that there may sometimes be overriding Reasons of State before which even the truth must bow. Certainly, all actual states are prepared to withhold information and even actively to deceive when their vital interests are perceived to be at stake.[12]

Nevertheless, there are great dangers in this principle, as Plato himself recognises. He likens falsehood to a strong 'medicine', the administration of which should be entrusted only to doctors (389b). For Plato, the Rulers are experts, like doctors, and so he is relatively sanguine about granting them the right to lie when they deem it necessary. If one is less convinced than Plato of the expertise of rulers, and if, like Mill and Popper, one believes that the interests of rulers and people may well diverge, then one will be more conscious than Plato of the dangers of leaving rulers unsupervised, and more concerned to protect people against the abuse of power. However, these are issues about who should determine when lying is necessary, not about whether or not it may sometimes be so.

Guide to Further Reading

Annas, *Introduction to Plato's* Republic, Chapter 4, has a good discussion of the issues raised by this section. Nettleship, *Lectures*, Chapter 5, gives a useful brief account of Plato's educational ideas. He covers similar ground at greater length in *The Theory of Education in Plato's* Republic.

Mill, *On Liberty*, Chapters 1–2, gives a celebrated and eloquent defence of freedom of thought and discussion which contains important explicit and implicit criticisms of Plato. Popper attacks Plato for advocating censorship and propaganda in *The Open Society*,

---

[12] Mill *should* be committed to this view, since his utilitarian approach implies that telling the truth, like any other activity, is good only in so far as it promotes the greatest happiness of the greatest number. However, in *On Liberty*, Ch. 2, he appears to maintain that liberty of expression should be absolute.

Volume I. His criticisms are discussed in the articles collected in J. R. Bambrough (ed.), *Plato, Popper and Politics*.

5 Communism and the Individual
(III.415d–IV.427c)

The Guardians must be entirely devoted to their task, which is ruling in the social interest. Education and upbringing alone are not sufficient to ensure this. The danger is that even the most carefully selected and trained Rulers will develop private interests and loyalties, and pursue these at the expense of the interests of the wider community. Private property and the family are the main focus for such private interests and loyalties. Plato's proposal for dealing with them is radical: they must be abolished.

Rulers and Auxiliaries are to lead a life of austere simplicity. They are to have no possessions beyond the bare essentials. They are forbidden to own property, handle money or accumulate wealth. They do not have private dwellings, but live and eat communally 'like soldiers in a camp' (416e). These arrangements apply to the Guardians only. Among the Productive Workers extremes of wealth and poverty are to be avoided lest these become a source of division and conflict, but no specific economic measures are described.

For the Guardians, however, the abolition of private property is supposed to ensure that their first concern is for the social interest rather than for their own particular interests. It will

> prevent the dissension that starts when different people call different things their own, when each carts off to his own private house anything he can lay hands on for himself, and when each has his own wife and children, his own private joys and sorrows.[1]

---

[1] *Republic* 464c–d.

By converting private property into communal property,
Plato's hope is that it will become the object of common concern,
and a cause of social cohesion and solidarity rather than self-
ishness and strife. 'Our citizens ... are devoted to a common
interest, which they call *my own*; and in consequence entirely
share each other's feelings of joy and sorrow.' Plato uses the
organic analogy to explain his thinking. 'A well-run society [is]
like] the human body, in which the whole is aware of the feelings
of the part' (464a–b).

Similar considerations apply to the family. It is the focus
of powerful loyalties and attachments, distinct from, and potentially in competition with, those of the wider community. Plato
thus proposes to abolish the family among the Guardians. Mating
and parenthood are planned and organised for eugenic purposes.
Children are reared communally; they do not know the identity
of their biological parents; they are brought up to regard all fellow
citizens as their relations.[2] Plato's idea is to abolish particular
family attachments in order to transfer them to the wider
community. The whole community must become as one large
family, in which every member regards all others as family
relations.

Even the normally docile Adeimantus is provoked by these
startling proposals. The Guardians will not be made particularly happy by them, he objects. Plato has a characteristic and
telling reply. The purpose of his proposals, he reminds Adeimantus, is

> not to promote the particular happiness of a single class, but, so far as
> possible, of the whole community ... We are ... trying to contruct what
> we think is a happy community by securing the happiness not of a select
> minority, but of the whole.[3]

Plato compares the construction of an ideal society with painting
a statue, where the aim is not to reserve the most beautiful colours
for the most beautiful parts of the body, but to make 'the whole
beautiful by giving each part its proper colour' (420d). The aim
must be for the happiness and the good of the whole,

---

[2] See Ch. 8 below.
[3] *Republic* 420b–c.

and our Guardians and Auxiliaries must be compelled to act accordingly and be persuaded . . . that it is their business to perfect themselves in their own particular job; then our state will be built on the right basis, and, as it grows, we can leave each class to enjoy the share of happiness its nature permits.[4]

It may seem from this that the Guardians' happiness is being sacrificed for the good of the whole. Referring back to this passage a little later, however, Plato maintains that the Guardians will, in fact, achieve the greatest possible happiness in this way, and any Guardian who 'tires of the restraint and security of the ideal life we have drawn for him' will come to regret it (466b).[5]

Again what Plato is saying is best understood in terms of the analogy of society with a living organism. A doctor who is treating a particular part of the body, for example, must still be primarily concerned for the health of the body as a whole and not just for the well-being of the part, no matter how important the part may be; for the good of the whole is the precondition for the good of the parts. This is why the apocryphal headline 'operation successful but patient dies' is ultimately nonsensical. Likewise, the Guardians are supposed to govern in the interests not just of a particular section of the community, nor even of the majority, but of the whole. In so doing, however, they are not sacrificing their own happiness for the social interest. On the contrary, a well-functioning society is the necessary precondition for their happiness, and that of the other classes too.

Here, Plato's approach differs fundamentally from the modern utilitarian idea that politics and morals should promote 'the greatest happiness of the greatest number'.[6] This presupposes a situation of potential conflict between individuals in which the interests of the lesser number may have to be sacrificed for those of the greater. Plato does not accept that conflict in the community is inevitable. His aim is the good not just of the majority but of the whole.

---

[4] *Republic* 421b–c.

[5] See also 576b–578b. However, it becomes apparent that Plato is ambivalent about the ideal life for the Guardians, see pp. 128–30 below.

[6] Mill, *Utilitarianism*, contains the classic modern account of this doctrine, though he does not use precisely this phrase.

Communism: Ancient and Modern

In important respects, Plato's proposals to abolish private property and the family are the precursor of all communistic philosophies which see private property and sectional interests as the main causes of social strife and unhappiness and which seek a communal alternative. At the same time, there are fundamental differences between Plato's 'communism' – as these proposals are often called – and the modern variety.

In the first place, the aim of present-day communism is to end the economic exploitation and political subordination of the working class and to eliminate class divisions generally. Plato, by contrast, wants to strengthen class distinctions and social stratification. He wants to reinforce the power and control of the elite class of Guardians, and to ensure the subservience of the Workers. Indeed, it seems most likely that Plato's ideal state is founded on slavery. Although he does not state this explicitly, he makes a number of casual and passing references to slavery in which it is clearly implied.[7] Slavery, it should be noted, was common and accepted in the ancient world.

A further point of contrast is that whereas modern communism equates betterment with economic development, Plato is deeply hostile to any increase of material wealth. Modern communism, says Barker,

> demands an equal division of material goods for the sake of an equal diffusion of material happiness. Plato demands an equal abnegation ... Where modern socialism is positive, Plato is negative: while in its tenets there is something of hedonism, in his there is only too much asceticism.[8]

Plato is not concerned with issues of inequality and exploitation; his sole concern is to ensure that the Guardians are not diverted from their allotted task: they must devote themselves fully to the community and its interests. Plato's communism is more like that of a medieval monastery in which the monks live communally, without families or material possessions, so that they will not be distracted from their service to God.

---

[7] See esp. 431c (quoted below p. 59), 433d, 469c, and G. Vlastos, 'Does Slavery Exist in Plato's *Republic*?'

[8] Barker, *Political Thought of Plato and Aristotle*, p. 138.

Nevertheless, modern communists and Plato agree that private property and the family are the main causes of social strife, and that private property at least should be abolished. Modern arguments about these ideas often centre around the question of whether private property is a universal and inviolable 'natural right'. Such moral absolutes are foreign to ancient Greek thought which focuses rather on the moral and social consequences of activities and institutions.

These are the issues that Aristotle considers in his *Politics*, in what still remains one of the most acute discussions of Plato's communistic proposals. Aristotle criticises Plato for holding that private property is responsible for divisions and ills in the community. These are not due to the absence of communal ownership, he maintains, 'they arise out of the depravity of human character'.[9] Indeed, Aristotle questions the view that the moral effects of private property are invariably harmful. Though it may promote self-interest, not all self-interest is to be condemned, only 'excessive' self-interest. Private property gives people the opportunity to exercise the virtues of generosity and self-discipline (especially of men towards women).

Conversely, Aristotle argues, it is wrong to think that common ownership will automatically foster a concern for the common interest.

> The greater the number of owners, the less the respect for common property. People are much more careful of their personal possessions than of those owned communally: they exercise care over common property only in so far as they are personally affected.[10]

These are perceptive observations about the ways in which people actually behave; but it does not necessarily follow that they should be taken to refute Plato's proposals. Plato is not talking about the way people actually are: he is presenting a vision of an ideal society in which, he believes, our current possessive and self-interested nature would be changed. The possibility of this cannot be refuted simply by describing the unideal present.

[9] *Politics* 1266b.
[10] *Politics* 1261b.

Aristotle's view that human depravity rather than private property is responsible for social division also needs to be questioned. Plato seems nearer the truth when he argues that our characters are affected by the social system, and that private property makes people self-interested, competitive and aggressive. Surprisingly, he has a supporter here in Margaret Thatcher. One of the benefits that she claims for the privatisation of public property is that it encourages individual enterprise and competition. Plato agrees about the effect, but draws the opposite lesson: this is the very reason why private ownership should be eliminated and property communalised.

Aristotle also argues that common ownership will lead to discontent and undermine the incentive to work, because the lazy and the hard working are rewarded equally.[11] But is it true that people work only when they have a material incentive to do so? Plato wants his Guardians to govern not for material gain but for the good of the community. Marx, too, believed that in a communist society people will work not because they are paid but because work has become 'life's prime want'.[12]

Equalitarian experiments and attempts to encourage voluntary labour in the early years of the Russian and Chinese revolutions had mixed results. Again, however, we need to recall that these were inspired by views about how human nature and society ideally should be.[13] These ideas cannot be ruled out solely on the basis of empirical observations of how people actually are. Ever since Plato, utopian thinkers have held such views knowing full well that human beings are not like this, but inspired by the belief that, with suitable social changes, they could become so.

Society and the Individual

Plato's vision is of a united community in which each individual relinquishes all private interests, and identifies completely with the whole. At least, this is what Plato envisages for the Guardian class. He does not explain why he does not extend these proposals to the

---

[11] *Politics* 1263a.
[12] K. Marx, 'Critique of the Gotha Programme', p. 24.
[13] See, e.g., V. I. Lenin, 'A Great Beginning'.

Productive Workers. Apart from his usual disinterest in their lives, the reason is perhaps that he does not believe they possess the necessary rational capacities for such renunciation. In any case, for the Guardians at least there is no private sphere: property and all other interests are shared and common; no area of life is separate from the collective life of the community.

These ideas are among the most controversial in the whole of Plato's work. More than any others, they give rise to the charge that Plato is the enemy of individuality. He is accused of subordinating the individual to the collective, of eradicating all privacy and protection for the individual against the community and state, and thus of justifying an intrusive and oppressive totalitarianism.[14]

Without doubt there is a solid basis to these charges. By abolishing private property and the family, Plato does seek to eliminate the private sphere. Every aspect of individual life, including sexual relations and the upbringing of children, is subject to communal control. In that sense, his ideal republic is, indeed, a form of totalitarianism.

Whether and in what sense it involves subordinating the individual to the collective raises more complex issues, however. Again, there is truth to the charge. Most clearly, Plato is prepared even to sacrifice the individual for the sake of the community when there is a fundamental clash of interests between them. Thus he advocates that the incurably sick – those who are 'no use either to [themselves] or society' – should be left to die (407c–408b). Serious and unreformable criminals should be executed (410a).

Plato's attitude to the ill is callous and inhuman by modern standards. However, such attitudes are not uncommon in less economically developed societies which cannot support the burden of the sick on the community, and would perhaps have been less shocking to his contemporaries than they are to modern readers. The practice of abandoning sickly infants at birth was not unknown among the ancient Greeks.

These observations may modify our judgement of Plato, but they do not justify his philosophy for the modern reader. Many will feel that what is lacking in it is any notion of the sanctity of

---

[14] These criticisms are forcefully and influentially expressed in Popper, *The Open Society*, Vol. I.

human life or thought that the individual possesses absolute and 'inalienable' rights. Moreover, these ideas – which are central to a great deal of modern moral thought – are not simply absent from Plato's philosophy, they are positively excluded by it. The view that the individual has absolute rights is incompatible with the analogy of society with an organism which is at the basis of Plato's account of the place of the individual in society.

The individual is essentially a social being and hence, Plato believes, like an organ of the body. An organ is not self-sufficient; it cannot function on its own; whereas the body can often survive without some of its organs, even though its functioning is impaired. An organism thus has an interest which is distinct from that of its separate parts. If an organ of the body becomes incurably diseased it may be necessary to sacrifice it to preserve the health of the body as a whole. A gangrenous limb may need to be amputated, for example. Malignant growths must be excised for the same reason. The interest of a part has no absolute claim. The interests of the whole must take precedence over it whenever there is a clash between them.

Such cases are the exception, however. When the body is in a normal and healthy condition, there is no fundamental conflict between the parts and the whole. Likewise, in a well-ordered society, Plato believes, there is no essential conflict between the individual and the community. Unlike the Sophists and other individualist philosophers he does not regard the demands of society and the interests of the individual as necessarily opposed. All individuals are members of the community and as such they share in the common social interest. There is no need, Plato therefore believes, for a private sphere or individual rights to protect the individual against the community or against other individuals. Indeed, he sees a separate private sphere as a seedbed for disunity and conflict, and that is why he wants to abolish it.

Although the collective interest does take precedence over the individual interest in the event of conflict between them, Plato's essential point is that they need not clash and, in ideal conditions, they will not do so. However, in the unideal conditions of the real world, conflicts between the individual and society are a frequent and familiar fact. In the real world, therefore, the question does arise of how the individual, and minorities of individuals, can be protected from the tyranny of the 'community', or rather the majority of it. This is a vital issue which Plato's philosophy – with its focus so fixed on the ideal – simply does not recognise, and which has been brought to the fore in modern political thought, particularly by Mill's *On Liberty*.

Nevertheless, it is wrong to accuse Plato of denying or seeking to crush individuality. What he does deny is the individualistic account of it. In its place he presents an account of individuality as essentially social. And his ideal society, he maintains, is one in which individuality is developed and realised to the full. For Plato's view is that the self, being essentially social, can develop and realise itself fully only in and through society – the highest life for the individual is the common, the collective, life. As Barker puts it,

> the individual is narrowest when he stands by himself, and widest when he exists and acts as a part, identifying himself with the interests of the whole body of which he is a part. The wider the whole of which the individual can act as a part, the greater ... is his individuality.[15]

Plato's philosophy is best seen as a form of communitarianism. His elimination of a separate private sphere is not intended to suppress the individual. His vision is of a united and harmonious community with which the individual is perfectly identified, and in which the individual has the full opportunity to develop and be realised. This is the ideal which Plato spells out in his account of justice, which we shall come to presently.

I have gone out of my way to defend Plato's treatment of the concept of individuality and try to bring out what is valuable in it, because the political and philosophical climate has been so hostile to it in recent years. However, it also has serious deficiencies which cannot be ignored. Plato's focus on ideal conditions means that he is oblivious to the problems which arise in the real world when individual and society conflict. Thinking in terms of individual rights, by contrast, highlights these issues, though it is not the only way of doing so, nor is it without problems of its own.

In any case, for better or worse the notion of rights is quite foreign to Plato. His stress is on the idea that we are social

---

[15] Barker, *Political Thought of Plato and Aristotle*, p. 154.

creatures who can thrive and develop only in community with others. Unfortunately, however, he maintains this idea in a thoroughly one-sided way. He wants the individual to be *totally* identified with the community. He will tolerate the development of individuality only in so far as it accords with the demands of a very authoritarian society. He treats the individual *purely* as a member of society, simply as a member of a class.

Thus, although he does not deny individuality, he has an extremely limited and restricted conception of it. He sees any autonomy on the part of individuals, any deviation from their social roles, as a diminution of individuality and a threat to social cohesion. As we have seen, commercial forces, and the individualism they brought with them, were changing Greek society rapidly in Plato's time. Plato sees only the negative side of these changes. For him they mean only the destruction of customary ways and the dissolution of the traditional order. His plan to abolish private property and the family are designed to counter these forces. With the benefit of historical hindsight, however, we can see that he was wrong to regard them only in a negative light, wrong to believe that community is possible only if all individual autonomy is suppressed.

Plato is not hostile to individuality as such, I have been arguing, rather he has a social conception of it. The same is true of modern communism. This may come as a surprise to those whose image of it is formed by cold war stereotypes, but it is true nevertheless. Marxism is a philosophy of individual development and self-realisation. Marx, like Plato, criticises the individualist view that society is intrinsically hostile to the individual, and that individuality can develop only in the private sphere, protected from communal pressures (whether by social means or through the magical powers of Gyges' ring). For both Plato and Marx agree that the individual is essentially social and that individuality can develop only in and through society.

However, they have very different conceptions of the nature of individuality and of the sort of society which fosters it. According to Plato, as we have seen, there are natural human differences which suit different individuals for different tasks. The highest realisation for each individual comes from concentrating on the task for which their abilities naturally suit them. Plato's ideal society is to be rigidly divided into different classes accordingly. Marxism, by contrast, rejects this idea of natural human inequality and difference. In common with other modern forms of socialism it envisages the possibility of a classless society in which specialisation and the division of labour are overcome and in which each individual can develop their talents without social limits or restraints in a universal and all round way.

Guide to Further Reading

Plato's communism is well discussed by Barker, *Political Thought of Plato and Aristotle*, Chapter 3 Section 6, and *Greek Political Theory*, Chapter 10. Aristotle's criticisms of it are in *Politics* II.i–v.

The view that Plato subordinates the individual to the state in ways comparable to modern totalitarianism is forcefully and influentially expressed in Popper, *The Open Society*, Volume I. Bambrough (ed.), *Plato, Popper and Politics*, contains articles discussing Popper's position. Marx's views on communism and individuality are best to be found in Marx and Engels, *The German Ideology*, Part I.

6 Justice in Society (IV.427d–434d)

Having sketched out his picture of the ideal society, Plato is now in a position to give at least a preliminary answer to the main question of the *Republic*, what is justice? A fuller and more precise account, he suggests, requires the 'Theory of Forms', presented only later in Book VI. However, what comes later is hazy and allegorical as an account of justice. Important though the Theory of Forms is in other respects, it adds little specific detail to our understanding of the nature of justice. The account in the present section is the most detailed that we get.

Following the method already laid down, Plato first considers justice in society (in the present section) then in the individual (see Chapter 7). The specific arguments by which he reaches his principle of social justice are weak and unconvincing. However, the conception of the just society that emerges is of the first importance. It suggests a way of thinking about social issues which has been influential ever since.

Plato's argument runs as follows. The society that he has been describing is the ideal society. It must therefore have the four cardinal virtues: wisdom, courage, self-discipline and justice. If he can locate the first three of these, he then maintains, it will be obvious by elimination where the fourth – justice – lies.

This procedure is highly questionable. Plato simply asserts, without argument, that there are these four main virtues. The list appears to derive from the popular morality of the time. Again without argument, Plato assumes that his list of social virtues is complete and exhaustive. Moreover, he treats each virtue as if it was a clear-cut and readily identifiable quality. He then proceeds on the assumption that they can then be eliminated one by one, like suspects from a criminal enquiry, until only one is left, which must therefore be the one we were seeking.

Moral qualities are not like this. They are not the kind of thing that can be identified and counted as Plato's method requires. There is a great deal of disagreement about every aspect of their nature, and even about their very existence. Plato's dialogues themselves make it clear that such disagreements are not just a modern phenomenon. One cannot help but feel that Plato already has his suspect marked out in advance.

Wisdom (428d–429a)

What does it mean to attribute wisdom to a society? As Plato points out, there are many kinds of wisdom in society. Carpenters and farmers, for example, have knowledge of their particular crafts; but, says Plato, a society would not be judged wise merely on account of having such individuals in it. The knowledge involved in practical crafts is merely particular knowledge for particular purposes. The kind of knowledge we are looking for is universal knowledge, philosophical knowledge – knowledge of the social Good, of the social interest. This is the kind of knowledge which only the Guardians possess.

Indeed, Plato goes out of his way to insist that those who have such knowledge constitute the 'smallest' social group, the elite of Rulers. The rest, he implies, can use their intelligence only in relation to their own concerns and to further their own interests. Plato thus displays a typically aristocratic disdain for practical knowledge. This contrasts strikingly with the pride that a modern industrial society typically takes in its engineering and technological achievements.

However, Plato is on stronger ground when he argues that for a society to be wise, it is not sufficient for it simply to contain within it a number of wise individuals. Their presence may have little effect on how the society is run or on its overall character. For the society to be wise, it must be ruled by wise individuals who exercise their knowledge on behalf of the whole.

Courage (429a–430c)

Plato makes similar points about courage as a social virtue. There are different kinds of courage, he maintains, but 'true' courage is a product of the Guardians' education. It is distinct from mere bravado in the face of physical danger, which can be exhibited even by 'animals and slaves' (430b). It is something more like steadfastness of character.

Indeed, so strongly does Plato stress knowledge of the distinction between real and merely apparent dangers as the foundation of true courage, that he ends up by seeming to imply that only the Rulers who have received a higher education are truly brave. Unfortunately, however, this conflicts with the view which he is just about to defend, that the society is brave because of its Auxiliaries.

Thus he goes on to argue that society as a whole is brave, not simply because it contains some individuals who are brave in this special Platonic sense, but because of the social role that these individuals play. Society is brave only if its Auxiliaries are brave, since it is they who have the role of defending it in the face of threats and dangers.

What, then, does it mean to attribute a quality such as wisdom or courage to a society? A society can be said to have such qualities only if it contains wise or courageous members. Thus when we say that a society has certain moral qualities, like wisdom or courage, we are saying something about the qualities of the individuals within it. On the one hand, we are not just saying that it contains individuals with these qualities. Claims about the qualities of a society are not simply reducible to statements about the qualities of individuals within it, as individualist thinkers suggest. On the other hand, we are not attributing these qualities to some mysterious entity 'over and above' the individuals who compose the society. For a society is not some additional entity over and above the individuals who compose it. When we attribute moral qualities to it, we do so in virtue of the fact that certain individuals within it are performing certain social roles, that they are exercising certain qualities in the context of the whole and on behalf of the whole.

Self-discipline (430d–432b)

Similar points apply in a more complex way to the next virtue that Plato identifies, self-discipline. This is one translation of *sōphrosunē*, otherwise translated as 'moderation' or 'temperance'. It is one of the key virtues in ancient Greece.[1]

Reversing his usual method in this instance, Plato explains the social virtue of self-discipline by reference to the individual case. In an individual, self-discipline is 'a kind of order, a control of certain appetites and desires', a kind of 'self-mastery' (430e). These phrases are paradoxical. They suggest that one can be both master of oneself and at the same time subject to oneself. Yet 'there is only one person in question throughout' (431a).

Anticipating an important line of thought that is spelled out at greater length in the next section (435e–441c), Plato argues that we can make sense of the situation if we assume that there are different parts of the personality or self (*psuchē*).

> When the naturally better element controls the worse then the man is said to be 'master of himself', as a term of praise. But when (as a result of bad upbringing or bad company) the smaller forces of one's better element are overpowered by the numerical superiority of one's worse, then one is adversely criticized and said not to be master of oneself.[2]

There is an analogy with society, as Plato has been hinting with his talk of 'smaller' and 'more numerous' elements. A society is self-disciplined when its 'better part rules the worse' (431b), in the sense that 'the desires of the less respectable majority are controlled by the desires and the wisdom of the superior minority' (431c–d). The 'less respectable majority', we are told, comprises 'children, women and slaves' as well as the 'majority of so-called freemen' (431c).

The hierarchical and inequalitarian character of Plato's social philosophy is fully evident here. His ideal society is divided into a small group of Rulers, and a large mass who appear to have no other virtue to contribute than their 'self-discipline', their docile acceptance of their subordinate social position.

---

[1] Self-discipline is the main topic of Plato's earlier dialogue, the *Charmides*, where some of the difficulties of defining it are demonstrated.

[2] *Republic* 431a–b.

A deep ambivalence runs right through the *Republic* about the character of the society thus envisaged. At times, Plato seems to believe that society is made up of a volatile and unruly mass who must be kept in place from above by a small elite of Rulers and armed Auxiliaries. The Productive Workers lack the rational capacity to govern themselves, discipline must be imposed upon them from above. This view is particularly evident in Plato's parallel picture of the role of the appetites in the individual self, as we shall see. In his more benign and idealistic moments, however, Plato suggests that the Workers are naturally deferential. They have sufficient rationality and good will to recognise the superior wisdom of their betters and to discipline themselves accordingly.[3]

The latter view is particularly stressed in the present section. Plato explicitly argues that a well-ordered society must be founded on cooperation and consent. Unlike wisdom and courage, he insists, the virtue of self-discipline is not located in one class alone. It is a matter of how the rulers and the ruled are related to each other. It involves a 'kind of concord' or 'harmony' between all the classes of society. A self-disciplined society is one in which all concur about who is to rule and who is to be ruled. Thus, the virtue of self-discipline is not identified with one class in particular, but must exist in all classes.

Nevertheless, the social structure that Plato envisages is hierarchical and unequal, and the virtue of self-discipline is exhibited very differently in the different classes. The 'worse' elements of society – as Plato has no hesitation in calling them – accept their lowly place and defer to the rulers whom they regard, and who regard themselves, as their natural superiors and natural leaders.

The language of 'concord' and 'cooperation' may seem inappropriate in such unequal conditions. The mere fact that the lower orders do not rise up in revolt proves nothing, it will be said: such talk confuses voluntary consent with acquiescence to force. In

---

[3] Williams describes this ambivalence in Plato unsympathetically but not inaccurately as follows. 'There have been those who thought that the working classes were naturally of powerful and disorderly desires, and had to be kept in their place. There have been those who thought they were good-hearted and loyal fellows of no great gifts who could recognize their natural superiors and, unless stirred up, keep themselves in their place. There can have been few who thought both. Plato in the *Republic* comes close to being one such.' ('The Analogy of City and Soul in Plato's *Republic*', p. 204)

criticising the Sophist account of human nature, Plato specifically rejects this view. Social behaviour is not based only on the threat of force and fear of punishment, as Glaucon suggests with the story of Gyges' ring. All community involves a degree of voluntary consent: the social order would be impossible without it. Even slaves (when they are not in a state of revolt) in a sense consent to their condition, in that they accept it and cooperate in it. It is consent and cooperation in this sense which is involved in Plato's notion of self-discipline.[4]

Justice (432b–434d)

Now that we have identified the first three social virtues, the fourth, justice, is supposed to be clear to see. After a rather tiresome charade of hunting about for it, Plato announces that it was there in front of us 'all the time'. Justice, he maintains, resides in the original principle of specialisation based on the natural division of labour, that each person should perform only the one job for which they are naturally suited. Each member of the community should 'do his own work' and 'mind his own business' (433a–e).

Earlier, in Book II, Plato puts this forward as an economic principle. Now he extends it to become a general political and moral principle. Indeed, at this point Plato pretty well abandons any application it may have in the economic sphere. It does no great harm, he admits, if a builder and a shoemaker exchange jobs. What really concerns Plato is the maintenance of the division of labour between classes. His language could hardly be stronger. If someone who 'belongs by nature to the class of artisans and businessmen' tries to become a Guardian, this is 'the worst of evils' and 'spells destruction to our state' (434b–c).

To the modern reader, phrases such as 'doing one's own work' or 'minding one's own business' all too readily suggest an individualist philosophy of self-interest. Plato's meaning is very different. Individuals are not isolated atoms; they are members of a community. In carrying out their own particular and specialised

[4] However, Rousseau may be right to question the validity of such consent. 'Slaves lose everything in their chains, even the desire of escaping from them' (*Social Contract*, I.ii).

tasks, they are at the same time fulfilling an essential function in the social whole. They are not only pursuing their own interests, they are also acting socially and fulfilling the social interest.

In this way, the just society is like a healthy organism in which the parts carry out their particular functions and, in so doing, also work together cooperatively for the good of the whole. Similarly, in a just society each member has a different but equally essential contribution to make, and all work together cooperatively for their own good and for the social good. The just society is thus a well-functioning, a happy, a harmonious, a healthy society. Conversely, an unjust society is one beset by internal conflicts – a divided, unhappy, unharmonious, sick society.

Plato was originally challenged to define justice and show that it is good in itself. This is the first stage of his reply. This is Plato's account of justice in society. But is it really about justice? Plato's definition does not appear to coincide with the ordinary meaning of the term, which involves the idea that people 'should not take other people's belongings or be deprived of their own', and such like. However, Plato insists that the ordinary notion of justice is encompassed within his account (433e). It is important that he should demonstrate this. If he is not using the term 'justice' in the sense understood by Thrasymachus, Glaucon and Adeimantus, then he is not responding to their challenge, but defining a different notion. This is a serious problem for Plato, particularly when he comes to explain his notion of justice in the individual, and I shall return to it at greater length in the next chapter.

The Idea of a Harmonious Society

In assessing these ideas it is useful to distinguish two aspects of Plato's philosophy: its inequalitarianism and its communitarianism. Both aspects are evident in Plato's account of justice in society.

The inequalitarianism of Plato's social philosophy is undoubted. Plato's vision is of the working together of inherently unequal and hierarchically organised classes. As Popper says,

> Plato identifies justice with the principle of class rule and class privilege.
> For the principle that every class should attend to its own business means,

briefly and bluntly, that *the state is just if the ruler rules, if the worker works, and if the slave slaves.*[5]

Each individual is a mere cog with a place in the larger social machine to which it is entirely subordinated.

The notion of social 'place' which runs through Plato's philosophy is a dated and feudal-sounding notion. It has conservative and elitist implications which few modern thinkers would wish to defend. Separated from this, however, the ideal of a harmonious community is still enormously influential. The vision of a society in which every individual plays an essential role continues to be at the basis of much radical and utopian social thought. The Rousseauian idea of an autonomous, self-governing community of equal citizens and the ideal of a classless communist society are among its contemporary incarnations. Moreover, this way of thinking about society often employs the organic analogy first spelled out by Plato. For the ideal is conceived of as a harmonious, healthy and unalienated community, by comparison with which contemporary conditions can be criticised as sick and alienated.

The Ideal as a Critical Concept

The notion of a just and harmonious society is put forward by Plato as an ideal. It is a vision of how things *ought* to be rather than how in fact they are. Plato is clear and explicit about this. What is less clear is how this ideal is to be applied in our thinking about actually existing, unideal societies. There are two quite different ways of reading Plato's philosophy on this issue.

If actually existing society is regarded as an approximation to the ideal, if the present social order is pretty much as it ought to be, then the message of Plato's philosophy is: fulfil your allotted task, conform, keep your place, submit yourself to the demands of society and defer to the powers that be. It is this depressing and conservative reading that Popper appears to adopt when he accuses Plato of advocating the subordination of the individual to the state. If this was Plato's sole message his philosophy would be of little interest; indeed, it would be difficult to understand its enduring influence.

---

[5] *The Open Society*, Vol. I, p. 90 (italics in original).

Alternatively, however, the prevailing order may be regarded as far from ideal. In that case, the idea of a harmonious society becomes a standard by which it can be criticised. As we know, Plato was deeply critical of the Athens of his time; and there is every reason to believe that this was Plato's own approach.

This critical reading makes Plato into a far more interesting and worthwhile philosopher than the conservative interpretation suggested by Popper. It suggests a philosophy which has important application in the modern world. For society today is far from the harmonious ideal that Plato's philosophy envisages. It is disordered and disunited, full of tension and conflict. It has no use for millions of its members who are unemployed and thus effectively denied any useful social role. Countless others are condemned to futile and alienating forms of work which neither employ their abilities adequately nor contribute anything of real value to the community. In this context the Platonic ideal of a harmonious community, so far from being a philosophy of mere conformity, provides a standard for a radical and far-reaching critique of prevailing conditions.

Individual Interests and the Social Interest

For some, these are among the most important and inspiring aspects of Plato's philosophy. Others, however, recoil from them with horror. According to Isaiah Berlin, for example, the notion of a 'final harmony' is a 'metaphysical chimera', a dangerous creation of false theory. Like the Sophists, he maintains that, in the real world, people participate in society as independent individuals whose interests inevitably conflict and cannot be harmonised. 'The world that we encounter in ordinary experience is one in which we are faced with choices between ends equally ultimate, and claims equally absolute, the realization of some of which must inevitably involve the sacrifice of others.'[6]

No doubt, clashes of individual interests are a feature of all actually existing societies. Berlin is right to remind us of the imperfections of the real social world. Plato was not unaware of them as his account of 'imperfect' societies in Books VIII–IX

[6] I. Berlin, 'Two Concepts of Liberty', p. 168.

shows. In general, however, he is perhaps open to the criticism that he focuses too much on the ideal and pays too little attention to the problems of justice in the real world.

What is more questionable, however, is whether Berlin is right to regard this imperfect reality as the only possibility, as the inevitable nature of things. This ultimately is what Plato is questioning. The main purpose of his philosophy is not to analyse the actual world and its problems, but to offer a vision of an ideal, of what could be and what ought to be. Anyone who has glimpsed that vision will find it difficult to remain content with Berlin's dark view that social conflict is inevitable, and that all we can hope for is a more or less satisfactory compromise between competing individual interests.

Berlin's view, like that expressed by Glaucon, is based upon the individualist assumption that individual interests are irreconcilably in conflict. Plato's philosophy is a sustained critique of this view. As we have seen, he argues that people are essentially members of a community. As such they share a common interest. A just society, he maintains, is a harmonious society in which the rulers act as guardians of the common interest. For Plato the individual is essentially social. As a member of the community, the individual is bound up with others; his or her interests are connected with those of others and with that of the community as a whole. The self is social, and *so too therefore is self-interest*. Not only the social interest but also individual interests are served when individuals are 'doing their own work'; for then they are using their abilities to the full, doing what best suits them; and this is possible only in the context of a community. Or so Plato believes.

The crucial point, however, is that Plato, unlike the individualist philosophers that he opposes, does not regard individual and social interests as necessarily opposed. Ideally, in a just society, they can work in harmony. In short, in Plato's vision of the ideal society, neither the collective nor the individual is mere means for the other: *both* are equally satisfied. As Nettleship puts it,

> On the one hand no soul is self-sufficient, but each requires the help of society, and on the other hand every soul can contribute something to the social whole of which it forms a part. It results from this that the ideal of human society is a collection of souls so organized that each may

contribute its best to the whole and get back from the whole what it most wants; everybody in such a society would do what he was best fitted to do, and the result would be that everybody would do both what was best for himself and what was best for others.[7]

The Ethics of Specialisation

As has been noted, Plato's ideal of a harmony between individual interests and the social interest lives on, but it takes a very different form in contemporary socialist thought. Plato envisages a cooperative working together of classes which remain distinct and separate. Modern socialism, by contrast, maintains that class differences inevitably lead to class conflict. A harmonious society can come about only with the elimination of class divisions and the creation of a classless society.

In this respect, the socialist picture of a harmonious society is the opposite of Plato's. This is particularly clear in Marx's philosophy. His vision of a communist society involves the elimination of the sort of division of labour which Plato seeks to entrench, in which each person sticks to the one particular specialised task. For Marx this is a characteristic feature of alienation, and the very antithesis of a harmony between individual and social interest.

> As soon as the distribution of labour comes into being, each man has a particular, exclusive sphere of activity, which is forced upon him and from which he cannot escape. He is a hunter, a fisherman, a shepherd, or a critical critic, and must remain so if he does not want to lose his means of livelihood; while in a communist society, where nobody has one exclusive sphere of activity but each can become accomplished in any branch he wishes, society regulates the general production and thus makes it possible for me to do one thing today and another tomorrow, to hunt in the morning, fish in the afternoon, rear cattle in the evening, criticise after dinner, just as I have a mind, without ever becoming hunter, fisherman, shepherd or critic.[8]

These conflicting ideas of the ideal society are rooted in different conceptions of human nature. As we have seen, Plato's view is that people are inherently different and limited in their

[7] *Lectures*, pp. 163–4.
[8] Marx and Engels, *The German Ideology*, p. 53.

capacities. They are therefore happiest when their activities are confined to the particular sphere which best suits them. Marx, by contrast, believes that the form human capacities take is moulded by society. Limited capacities are the product of limiting social conditions. Potentially at least, human beings are capable of developing in a universal fashion.

While many agree that excessive specialisation has damaging human effects, they would also reject Marx's approach as impossibly utopian, and side with Plato here on the grounds that 'jack of all trades master of none'.

Guide to Further Reading

Annas, *Introduction to Plato's* Republic, Chapters 5–6, has a full and useful discussion of the issues raised by this section. There are briefer treatments in Nettleship, *Lectures*, Chapter 7, and in Cross and Woozley, *Plato's* Republic, Chapter 5.

Popper's criticism of Plato's 'totalitarian' conception of justice is in *The Open Society*, Volume I, Chapter 6. His account is discussed in the articles collected in Bambrough (ed.), *Plato, Popper and Politics*.

Moral attitudes to the division of labour and the idea of all-around human development are discussed in Marx and Engels, *The German Ideology*, Part I. My own views on these issues are spelled out at greater length in *Marxism and Human Nature*, Chapter 2.

7 Justice in the Individual
(IV.434d–V.449a)

Plato's focus now shifts to the workings of the individual self or personality.[1] This section is one of the most important in the *Republic*. In it Plato gives his account of justice in the individual and thus responds to the initial challenge of Glaucon and Adeimantus, to define justice and show that it is valuable in itself. He does so by developing the analogy between the structure of society and the structure of the individual self, which is such an original and distinctive feature of the *Republic*. However, he is careful to make clear that he is using the analogy only to suggest a hypothesis and not as a conclusive argument (434e).

It has been established that there are three basic classes in society, and that society is just when each class is fulfilling its proper function. 'Transferring' these findings to the individual, we can reasonably hypothesise that there will be three analogous elements in the individual self. With a series of unusually elaborate and detailed arguments, Plato now tries to establish that the self is made up of three elements or parts – reason, spirit and the appetites – which correspond to the three social classes. He is then able to give an account of the virtues in the individual which parallels that which he gives of them in society.

The Division of the Self

Plato argues that the self is complex by appealing to the phenomenon of psychological conflict. He gives the example of a person

[1] As noted in the Preface, Plato's word here is *psuchē* which is usually translated as 'soul'; but since the Greek has no particularly religious or spiritual connotations I shall generally use the terms 'self' or 'personality' instead.

who is thirsty and wants to drink some water yet holds back because he rationally reflects that the water will be bad for him (437d–439c). Thirst, he insists, is a blind desire for drink. It must be distinguished from the desire for pleasure, health or any of the other goods I may hope to gain from drinking. The appetite itself is simply a craving for drink.

When I am thirsty but refrain from drinking, Plato now argues, some other force must be restraining me, and this restraining force must emanate from some other part of the self. His argument for this appeals to a version of the logical principle of non-contradiction, to the effect that 'one and the same thing cannot act or be affected in opposite ways at the same time in the same part . . . and in relation to the same object' (436b, 436e–437a). Specifically, the appetite for drink is being restrained by the reflections of the rational part of self. Plato thus argues that reason and the appetites must be regarded as distinct and separate parts of the self.

He now uses similar arguments to show that spirit must be distinguished both from reason and from the appetites. To demonstrate the first of these points he cites the story of one Leontion, who passed by some executed corpses lying on the ground and was both drawn to look at them and yet at the same time disgusted with himself for this feeling. According to Plato we must see his self-disgust as due to spirit, which is here in conflict with the appetites. This also shows how spirit can side with reason against the appetites. For just as in a well-ordered society the Auxiliaries are allied with the Rulers to govern the Workers, so in the self spirit is 'a third element, which, unless corrupted by bad upbringing, is reason's natural auxiliary' (441a).

Finally, it is also clear that spirit is distinct from reason, since the two can conflict as well. Moreover, Plato argues, children are often full of spirit from an early age, before reason has developed in them; and animals, too, can be spirited although they are not rational. These are further proofs that reason and spirit are distinct.

Arguments such as these have been reiterated by subsequent thinkers, most influentially in modern times by Freud. Like Plato, Freud also points to the fact of mental conflict in order to argue that the self is complex. Ultimately Freud, too, settles on a tripartite division, into id, ego and superego, though there are also considerable differences between their theories.

The very idea that the self has parts is often disputed. Descartes argues that the self, the 'I', is a simple and indivisible unity. Sartre criticises the Freudian theory of the unconscious in similar terms for dividing the 'psychic whole in two'.[2] He objects that Freud illegitimately treats the self as if it is a composite entity made up of separate and distinct parts. Can the same criticism be made of Plato?

Plato does not spell out what he means when he talks of the self having parts. In most places the language he uses is vague, perhaps deliberately so. At times he treats reason, spirit and the appetites as though they were separate persons who can agree or disagree (e.g. 442c–d). It would be wrong to take such talk too literally, however, particularly in the present section. The basic point he wishes to establish with the arguments here is that the self is complex. We cannot comprehend the contradictory character of human feelings unless we recognise that there is more than one source of motivation in the self. But these are different aspects of a single self not distinct entities. A notable implication of this view is that a unified and coherent self is not a universal and necessary feature of human psychology but rather a condition which can be more or less adequately achieved.

In short, the idea of divisions within the self can be defended philosophically. Indeed, as Plato was the first to argue, it is essential to think in these terms if we are to comprehend the complexities of human psychology and morality.

Reason, Spirit and the Appetites

Plato uses these arguments not only to establish that the self has three parts, but also to develop an account of the nature of these parts. This psychological theory is filled out further in Book IX, but it will be useful to summarise some of its main features here.

Reason: is the reflective and intelligent part of the self. It has two quite different functions. On the one hand, reason is the intellectual part of the personality which is responsible for understanding and the grasp of truth in both theoretical and practical matters. It

---

[2] Descartes, *Meditations*, VI; J.-P. Sartre, *Being and Nothingness*, p. 50.

is the philosophical part of the self in the widest sense, the part which gives us a love of knowledge. It is also the part which attracts us to what is harmonious and beautiful. Thus for Plato reason is not the inactive and purely deliberative faculty described by empiricist philosophers like Hobbes and Hume. It has a motivational force and characteristic activity of its own: the contemplation of truth, beauty and goodness in all their forms.

But reason also has a second and quite different role. It is the part of the self which has concern for the interests of the personality as a whole. The other parts care only for their own interests. The appetite of thirst, for example, strives only for drink, even if this is harmful to the organism as a whole. Reason is thus best fitted to govern the self (441e, 442c). Just as the Rulers together with the Auxiliaries rule over the producers, so reason with the help of spirit has the task of controlling the appetites and desires. In a well-ordered society, Plato says, the appetites should be the 'slaves' of reason (444b).

Hume deliberately inverts this when he says that 'reason is and ought to be the slave of the passions'.[3] For Hume believes that reason plays a role like that of a scientific advisor who gives expert opinion about the effects of different policies, but does not make policy (that is the job of the politicians). For Plato, by contrast, reason is active and in command of the personality, just as the Rulers rule the society by virtue of their wisdom and expertise.

Plato's view that reason has these two quite different functions is indicative of an ambivalence about the proper role of the philosopher which runs right through his philosophy, as we shall see more fully in due course (Chapter 11). At times he suggests that the best and happiest life for the philosopher is the contemplative life, but elsewhere he maintains that philosophers must engage in politics and use their skills to rule.

Spirit: (or, better, the spirited part of the self) encompasses a number of assertive and active aspects of the self. It is the part responsible for the ambitious and competitive side of the personality. It is also the part of the self which leads to righteous anger and indignation (as exhibited in the story of Leontion). Spirit plays

---

[3] Hume, *Treatise of Human Nature*, p. 415.

a less prominent role in Plato's psychology than the other two divisions of the self, and it has less resonance in modern psychological thought. With some justification it has been said that Plato is really giving a twofold account of the self, in which spirit plays the role of mere auxiliary to reason in its battle to keep the appetites in check.

The Appetites. Plato uses the term in a narrower and a wider way. In the narrower sense the appetites are a particular part of the self. The 'clearest examples' (437d), says Plato, are bodily desires – for food, drink, sex, etc., but they also include the desire for wealth as a means of satisfying these (436a). The appetites in this sense blindly seek their own satisfactions; they are multiple and disorderly. However, Plato also uses the term in a broader sense to mean a want of any kind. Thus towards the end of Book IX he speaks of reason and spirit as having their characteristic desires and activities which satisfy them.

In the present passage, Plato insists that desires in the narrow sense are blind and irrational cravings. In other places, however, he writes of the appetites as though an element of rationality is involved in them. Thus he describes how, in the self-disciplined personality, the appetites 'agree that reason should rule' (442c). This contradiction reflects a pervasive tension in Plato's moral and social thought. On the one hand, he is profoundly wary of the role of appetites in human life and wants to suppress them, sometimes it seems altogether. On the other hand, he recognises that the appetites are an ineliminable part of the self, and that the satisfaction of their necessary demands plays an essential part in human life and human happiness.

The Virtues in the Individual

Each self is a community in miniature, made up of three parts. These parts are differently developed in different individuals, and this is what distinguishes the different classes. Reason is most developed in the Rulers, spirit in the Auxiliaries, and the appetites in the Workers.

Plato's account of the nature of the virtues in the individual follows from this picture. An individual is wise when their personality is governed by its rational part, and courageous when spirit is dominant in the self. As with society, Plato presumes a natural inequality and hierarchy among the different parts of the self. Reason is the 'higher' and 'better' part and, with the assistance of spirit, it must keep the appetites in check. A person exhibits the virtue of self-discipline when the 'lower' part of their personality is controlled by the 'higher' part, so that no more than their essential needs, their 'necessary desires', are allowed to develop.

Finally, justice in the individual exists when all the parts are working harmoniously together, and each part is fulfilling its proper function in the context of the whole (441e). Thus the term 'justice' has the same meaning whether it is applied to society or the individual. Moreover, the analogy of justice and health continues to hold. Just as the body is healthy when its parts are functioning together harmoniously, so justice, says Plato, 'is a kind of mental health' (444d). Conversely, the self is unjust when it is divided by unresolved conflicts. Injustice in the individual, Plato maintains, is 'a kind of civil war' in the self; its result is 'indiscipline, cowardice, ignorance and ... wickedness of all kinds' (444b).

These are the terms in which Plato now replies to the initial challenge of Glaucon and Adeimantus to show that justice 'pays' and is good in itself. Since justice has been identified with harmony of the self it leads to happiness, and since it is a kind of health it is desirable for its own sake, quite irrespective of whatever external rewards it may bring. As Glaucon acknowledges, justice is thus clearly preferable to injustice and good in itself (445a).

The theory of the three parts of the self and the account of justice as psychological harmony are the central notions of Plato's moral thought. They are among the most important ideas in the whole dialogue. Ever since they were first advanced they have generated discussion and controversy. In the rest of this chapter I shall focus on some of the issues which have been central to recent debate.

Justice and Mental Health

Plato was the first thinker to conceive of moral issues in psychological terms, in terms of mental health and illness. The idea that justice in the individual consists in the harmony, the integrity, the health of the personality is Plato's great innovation in moral thought. This way of thinking about moral questions has been enormously influential in recent times. Particularly with the rise of psychoanalysis, psychological language has come to play a central role in contemporary moral thinking. The view that crime should be regarded as a form of sickness rather than as an evil is widely prevalent in the 'caring professions' and more generally. Terms like 'sane' and 'well-balanced', or 'neurotic' and 'disturbed' have become as much a part of ordinary moral discourse as the traditional language of 'virtue' and 'wickedness'.

This whole approach has its critics as well. Moral problems are quite different from medical ones, it is said. It is philosophically mistaken and morally objectionable to treat moral issues as psychiatric conditions about which there is expert medical knowledge and techniques of 'treatment'. This way of conceiving of moral problems denies the freewill and responsibility of the moral agent.

These arguments are deployed against Plato by Kenny. By treating moral problems as though they were medical ones, he argues, Plato is implying that the Guardians are, as it were, doctors of the soul. Plato regards them not as rulers who are making fallible moral and political judgements, but rather as experts who have objective knowledge about how to cure the individual and society of injustice by eliminating its causes. Instead of responding to people in moral terms – with praise and blame, reward and punishment – they are to be regarded medically as cases for treatment. This approach, Kenny argues, is dehumanising and potentially dangerous.[4]

Plato rejects such views. He does indeed believe that moral matters can be just as much the subject of objective knowledge as medical ones. This view runs right through the *Republic*. It is implied by the analogy of the Ruler with a doctor, navigator or shepherd in Book I, and it is justified at length in terms of the Theory of Forms in Books V–VII. For Plato, knowledge about human psychology and human nature must be the basis of a rational approach to moral and political issues. This is the naturalistic approach to moral questions. Contrary to what Kenny argues, it has a long and distinguished history in moral philosophy and there is much to be said for it.

---

[4] A. J. P. Kenny, 'Mental Health in Plato's *Republic*'.

In looking at moral and social matters, according to naturalism, we must try to understand the causes of people's behaviour and act upon these. Such matters should not be treated as entirely distinct and separate from moral questions, as philosophers in the Kantian tradition, like Kenny, suggest. The only basis for resolving questions about moral values is an understanding of human nature and what makes for human well-being and happiness. Plato calls such knowledge 'philosophy'; nowadays we would look equally to psychology, sociology and other forms of social science. Of course, it must be admitted that we do not know much yet about human psychology and social behaviour – our expertise in these areas is still very limited. But according to the naturalistic approach there is at least some relevant knowledge, and a rational approach to moral and social questions must be based upon it.

The Rejection of Hedonism

Plato's tripartite account of the self plays a central role in his reply to the Sophists. Underlying the Sophist position is a hedonistic account of human nature. The self is portrayed as a bundle of appetites; and happiness consists in their satisfaction to the maximum extent. This picture is evident in the story of Gyges' ring. If we are not held back by conventional morality, the story suggests, we will indulge all our desires without restraint. Likewise, Thrasymachus argues that tyrants are the happiest of people because they have unlimited powers to satisfy their appetites (see Chapter 2 above).

Such hedonism is initially attractive. However, Plato criticises the equation of happiness with pleasure throughout his work; and, on reflection, it is clear that Plato offers a deeper and more satisfactory account of happiness. A life geared only to the satisfaction of the appetites may bring a great deal of sensual pleasure; it may result in physical comfort and a sort of contentment; but it does not lead to true happiness. The appetites are only one aspect of the self. There are other parts to the self, the activity and satisfaction of which are also necessary for genuine human happiness (*eudaemonia*). For human beings are capable of satisfactions greater than those of the appetites; there are further and ultimately more worthwhile ends in human life. Happiness, properly so called, consists in the satisfaction of all aspects of our selves in an integrated and harmonious way.

This point is vividly made by Huxley in *Brave New World*. In many respects, this novel is a modern parody of the *Republic*; but at the same time it is an attack on simple hedonism of the kind that underlies the Sophist position. In this respect it backs up Plato's account of human nature. The novel portrays a future society, organised in a supposedly rational and scientific fashion and dedicated to the pursuit of happiness. Its inhabitants have been bred and conditioned from the time of their conception to accept without question the prevailing values and their allotted social positions (which are as unequal and hierarchical as in Plato). Pleasure is the main aim of life, and everything which stands in its way has been eliminated. Intelligent and critical thought is suppressed since it gives rise to doubt and discontent; art and literature (apart from the pornographic 'feelies') are banned since they stir up complex and troubling emotions. Whenever they arise, anxiety and other forms of pain are banished by means of the hallucinogenic drug 'soma'.

In short, the inhabitants of Huxley's world live lives of assured contentment with all their sensual desires satisfied. Yet this world is a nightmare. For all its discontents, present civilisation is preferable. One of the lessons of Huxley's story is surely this: if the appetites and sensual desires are taken for the whole of human nature then, indeed, the inhabitants of Brave New World would have the best of all possible worlds, with all their desires satisfied. Like Plato, however, Huxley is convinced that there is more to human nature than this.

Some accept these criticisms of hedonism yet still question Plato's approach. A major topic of recent debate in psychoanalysis is whether psychic health is a matter of harmony of the self or whether, as some postmodernists maintain, we should celebrate the diversity and multiplicity of the self and reject the very notion of psychic integration as illusory and repressive.

Plato is aware that the harmony he advocates is not the actual condition of the self, but that is not to say it is illusory: rather, it is an ideal. Moreover, he readily admits that it requires 'self-discipline', the restriction of desire. No doubt, Plato's attitude to the appetites is excessively negative and repressive. However, he insists, it is a mistake to imagine that happiness can be achieved by the mere absence of restraint. This is the condition of the 'democratic' personality described in Book VIII (558c–562a, see Chapter 12 below). Without the unifying direction of reason the self is fragmented and disordered. It haphazardly pursues any and every 'unnecessary' desire that it happens to feel and is never satisfied. An integrating influence is essential for happiness. These Platonic views are echoed and developed in some influential current strands of psychology.[5]

Does Plato's Reply Involve a Fallacy?

The initial challenge by Glaucon and Adeimantus is to show that justice is good in itself and not only as a means to external rewards. Plato answers here in Book IV by portraying justice as a sort of mental health, as the harmonious working together of the different parts of the self. This response, it is argued, involves a fallacy. Plato was challenged to defend the conventional concept of justice, but he replies by describing a quite different notion.

Justice as conventionally conceived is a social virtue which concerns the way we behave towards others. The Platonic notion of psychic harmony, by contrast, is an individual matter, defined purely with reference to the inner condition of the self. Plato himself emphasises this strongly when he insists that the 'real concern' of justice 'is not with external actions, but a man's inward self' (443c–d). To avoid a fallacy here, his critics maintain, Plato must demonstrate that these two conceptions of justice coincide. He must show that the harmonious personality will be just in conventional terms, and that the conventionally just person will have a harmonious personality.

Plato is not unaware of this issue. However, he makes only a minimal attempt to argue explicitly for the first of these claims, and none to establish the second. As regards the first, Plato asserts that a person with a harmonious self will not flout conventional principles of justice: he will not 'embezzle ... commit sacrilege or theft ... betray his friends or his country ... break a solemn

[5] See S. Frosh, *Identity Crisis*, for an account of the psychoanalytic discussion of these issues.

promise ... commit adultery, dishonour his parents, or be irreligious' (442e–443b). Plato appears to be assuming that such crimes are invariably due to the unconstrained operation of the appetites and self-interest (443b). But it is not at all clear that this is the case, or that people who commit such acts are always psychologically disturbed. On the contrary, some people seem able commit the most atrocious acts and yet remain remarkably undisturbed.

As to the converse claim, that the conventionally just person will necessarily have a harmonious self, Plato makes no attempt to establish this. Indeed, his whole position suggests that he rejects it, as we shall see in a moment. But before taking Plato's apparent failure to establish these claims as proof that the argument of the *Republic* is 'fallacious' we need to look more closely at Plato's purpose.

What is correctly pointed out by those who charge Plato with fallacy is that he does redefine the concept of justice. Indeed he does so in a most radical fashion. At the very outset of the dialogue, in the discussion with Cephalus and Polemarchus in Book I, Plato engages with the conventional conception – or rather conceptions – of justice and shows them to be confused, unclear and incoherent. Justice cannot adequately be defined in terms of outward rules of conduct (repaying debts or giving each person their due) as Cephalus and Polemarchus try to do. The conventional accounts of justice are unsatisfactory.

In a manner typical of the earlier 'Socratic' dialogues, Book I ends aporetically with this negative result. But by the time Plato came to write the *Republic* he wanted more than that. In the remainder of the dialogue he pushes beyond the bounds of the Socratic method to rethink and redefine the concept of justice. This involves changes and alterations to the conventional concept far beyond anything required for a mere clarification of the notion. For Plato is not simply analysing or clarifying the ordinary meaning of justice. He is revising, redefining, altering and changing the way justice is thought about.

In order for this new account of justice to be recognised as such and accepted as an account of justice, it must retain some continuity, some common ground, with the conventional notion it displaces. It must be recognisable as a form of the concept of justice and not seem to be some quite different notion. Plato attempts to establish this link in various ways. His account of justice in society as giving each element 'its due' and each 'doing its own' is designed to bring out the continuity between the conventional notion of justice and Plato's account of justice in society.[6] Plato then attempts to establish a link between these notions and the more radical innovation of justice as psychic harmony by insisting that the term 'justice' means exactly the same in relation to society as in relation to the individual: namely, each element doing its own job within the context of the whole (435b).

Without some continuity between the conventional and the Platonic senses of 'justice', the charge that Plato's response involves a fallacy would clearly be justified. However, an excessively narrow focus on the purely logical question of whether or not Plato has committed a fallacy here should not be allowed to obscure the wider significance of the changes that he is making in the ways we talk about justice. To appreciate this we need to see that the divergence of Plato's new account of justice from the conventional notion is also important. It allows the concept of justice to be used in a critical way, as a value by which to question and criticise the established order and its values.

Such revision in the use of terms is not peculiar to Plato, it is what all great philosophers accomplish. For a philosopher like Plato is no mere 'under labourer' who confines himself to analysing and clarifying existing concepts or 'ordinary usage', as adherents to the 'ordinary language' or analytic approach maintain is the task of philosophy. Or rather, even when Plato starts out on this path – as he does at the beginning of the dialogue – what he finds is that ordinary usage is confused and contradictory and that in attempting to bring order and clarity to it he is forced to innovate and refashion the way language is used.

In doing so, Plato is also reflecting the changes that were occurring in his social world. In the earlier Homeric period, the individual had a relatively fixed and given place and status within the social system. Moral values were closely tied to social roles. Virtue consisted in performing one's social role well. As this social structure loosened during the fifth century through the influence

---

[6] Cf. G. Vlastos, 'Justice and Happiness in the *Republic*'.

of commercial forces, moral values began to break free of specific social roles. It became possible to ask about the value of a role itself, or even of a whole society. Morality in its modern form, as a system of values relatively independent and separate from a particular social system, was coming into being.[7]

Plato is both registering these changes and creating them when he shifts the focus in the meaning of justice from outer behaviour to the inner state of the self, from social to individual, from relative to absolute. This is a radical and epoch-making shift of perspective – a veritable 'revaluation of values'.

It now becomes possible to ask about the justice of one's own society and one's own role in it, and one can criticize conventional values in moral terms. For now there are two quite different and distinct criteria with which to assess individual behaviour or social events in moral terms: a conventional standard which is relative to the existing social order, and a Platonic, absolute one. Laing has an image which well illustrates the difference.

> From an ideal vantage point on the ground, a formation of planes may be observed in the air. One plane may be out of formation. But the whole formation may be off course. The plane that is 'out of formation' may be abnormal, bad or 'mad' from the point of view of the formation. But the formation itself may be bad or mad from the point of view of the ideal observer. The plane that is out of formation may be also more or less off course than the formation itself.[8]

Plato attempts to establish such an 'ideal vantage point' through the Theory of Forms. With his revisionary accounts of justice as social harmony and harmony of the self, he is the first philosopher to produce a systematic and coherent theory of what it is for a society or an individual to be 'off course'.

In the ideal society that Plato envisages, there are no conflicts between these two sorts of criteria: the whole society is 'on course' and no one is 'out of formation'. For Plato's republic is designed as a society in which the just individual is fully realised and at home. But in the unjust and unideal conditions of the real world such conflicts exist. How then should the just person conduct themselves in an unjust world?

---

[7] See A. MacIntyre, *After Virtue*, Chs 10–11.
[8] R. D. Laing, *The Politics of Experience*, p. 98.

This issue touched Plato directly. He was deeply critical of the Athens of his day. Not long before writing the *Republic* he had seen its best and wisest person, his teacher and friend Socrates, tried and put to death unjustly. No doubt with this in mind, in a bitter and powerful passage, he compares a corrupt society with a ship of drunk and quarrelling sailors. In such a situation, he argues, the 'true navigator' will try to prevail as far as is possible. Otherwise, he (or she) should simply keep himself to himself and avoid being tainted by 'the general wickedness'.[9]

In sum: Plato does indeed redefine the notion of justice. He thus effects a profound shift in our understanding of the term. To see this only as a logical 'fallacy' in Plato's reply to the initial challenge, in the manner of many recent commentators, is to miss the epoch-making significance of this shift.

Guide to Further Reading

Useful commentaries on this crucial section are to be found in: Annas, *Introduction to Plato's* Republic, Chapters 5–6; Nettleship, *Lectures*, Chapter 7; and Cross and Woozley, *Plato's* Republic, Chapter 6.

For general discussion of the view that moral issues should be thought of in psychological terms, see T. S. Szasz, *Ideology and Insanity*, and S. Sayers, 'Mental Illness as a Moral Concept'. For specific application of these arguments to Plato as well as a full and useful summary of Plato's account of justice in the individual, see Kenny, 'Mental Health in Plato's *Republic*'.

The criticism that Plato's reply involves a fallacy is most influentially made in D. Sachs, 'A Fallacy in Plato's *Republic*'. See also R. Demos, 'A Fallacy in Plato's *Republic*?', Vlastos, 'Justice and Happiness in the *Republic*', and Annas (as above) for further discussion. A. MacIntyre, *A Short History of Ethics*, Chapters 2–6, and *After Virtue*, Chapters 10–11, give thought-provoking accounts of the historical background to Plato's work upon which I have drawn in this chapter.

---

[9] 496d, see pp. 98–9 below.

8 Women and the Family
(V.449a–V.471c)

Socrates has now spelled out his conception of justice. He is on the point of completing his reply to the initial challenge by considering the nature of injustice when he is interrupted by Polemarchus and Thrasymachus, who, it seems, have been silently present all along (there is no clear reason for their unexpected reappearance at this point in the dialogue). Before going any further, they insist, Socrates must explain and defend his proposal that women and children should be held 'in common' (424a). So begins a lengthy digression in which Plato confronts what he calls three great 'waves' of sceptical doubt. The first concerns the role of women, the second his proposals for marriage and the family, and the third his idea that the rulers of society should be philosophers. The dialogue eventually returns to the subject of injustice only in Book VIII (543a), where it resumes exactly where it breaks off here.

Plato's ideas about women and the family raise some topical issues. To appreciate properly their significance, however, it is necessary to understand something of the position of women in ancient Athenian society. This was one of almost complete exclusion from public life. Women were all but confined to the home and, when there were male visitors, to women's quarters within the home. Even shopping and other such errands were normally done by men or slaves. Women's role was restricted to the management of the household. Marriages were arranged. Women received no formal education. They were not citizens and had no voice in public affairs. It is symptomatic of this situation that the participants in Plato's dialogues are all men. The public realm was a male world. The only women who took part in it were foreign courtesans or *hetaerae* ('companions'). A modern comparison is with the position of women in some strict and traditional Islamic societies. This at least was the situation in Athens in Plato's time; in the earlier Homeric period and in Sparta at this time women played a considerably greater role in public life.

In this context Plato's proposals are extraordinarily radical. In some respects they remain radical even today. Plato argues that women should be given exactly the same upbringing and education as men, and that they should have equal access to all positions in society on the basis of merit, including ruling and even military service.

It has been argued that Plato's proposals about women and the family are deliberately meant to be regarded as 'preposterous', and that Plato intends them only 'ironically'.[1] There are no good grounds to believe this. They are taken seriously as Plato's views by no less an authority than Plato's pupil, Aristotle, who discusses them at length in *Politics*, Book II. Moreover, Plato's commitment to the equal treatment of women is evident in other of his dialogues.[2] There is nothing preposterous about this. Quite the contrary. It raises issues which have been central to the discussion of the role of women in society ever since.

The Position of Women

Plato introduces his proposals by appealing to an analogy between the Guardians and watchdogs which recurs throughout the *Republic*. Male and female watchdogs are both given the same training and expected to carry out the same functions, Plato observes: the Guardians of society should be treated similarly. To argue from what dogs are like in this way may seem crude and flippant, but it is not so. Plato is using a form of argument which still plays an important role in social thought. A great deal of contemporary discussion of sex roles relies on analogies with animal behaviour, and facts about animal behaviour are frequently cited as evidence for what is or is not 'natural'.

[1] A. Bloom, 'Interpretive Essay', p. 380. Cf. L. Strauss, *The City and Man*, p. 116.
[2] For example, *Meno*, in which Plato argues that virtue is the same in women and men, and *Timaeus*, which contains a summary of the *Republic*, including its proposals for women and the family.

Glaucon now raises an important objection. There are great natural differences between men and women, he observes. According to Plato's own principle of the natural division of labour they should surely have different social roles as a result. In response, Plato acknowledges that there are major differences between the sexes, particularly in the process of reproduction where 'the female bears and the male begets' (454e). However, he argues, not every natural difference is relevant to the question of what social role a person should perform. Some men are bald while others are not, but this is not relevant to their ability to perform their social roles. Similarly, Plato maintains, sexual differences are not socially relevant. Men and women should be educated equally and given the same social opportunities simply on the basis of their abilities.

Plato does not believe in that the sexes have equal abilities, however. In general, he maintains, women are the 'weaker' sex and less able 'at everything' (455d). Nevertheless, he says, there will be a good many women who are better at particular tasks than many men. And Plato does believe that the abilities of every individual should be developed and employed to the full. Thus, if a particular woman has the ability to be a Guardian then she should be selected and trained to be a Guardian. For Plato insists that 'there is . . . no administrative occupation which is peculiar to woman as woman or man as man; natural capacities are similarly distributed in each sex, and it is natural for women to take part in all occupations as well as men' (455d).

These principles have revolutionary implications, particularly when combined with the abolition of the family. They sweep away different sex roles. All jobs in society are open to all comers, and are to be filled purely on the basis of merit, regardless of sex. Plato's arguments for this are still controversial. They raise issues which have divided even the women's movement in recent years.

The mainstream of traditional feminism has long argued, like Plato, that the biological differences between the sexes are socially irrelevant. On this basis, it has fought for the equality of women with men in public life: in education, work and politics.[3] But these views are also challenged in some quarters. The Platonic approach,

---

[3] See S. de Beauvoir, *The Second Sex*, and B. Friedan, *The Feminine Mystique*, for classic statements of this position.

it is said, emphasises equality in a one-sided way and ignores the difference between the sexes. Plato's approach eliminates traditional sex roles and the distinctive characteristics and identities of women and men. According to writers like Strauss and Bloom, this is unnatural and impossible: it 'abstracts' from the body, it 'forgets' the realities of our physical being.[4]

This criticism is unjustified. Plato does not 'forget' the body: he specifically acknowledges that there are major physical differences between the sexes. And although he does 'abstract' from bodily differences, his argument is that these are not relevant to a person's ability to fulfil his or her social role. What is the criticism of this? It has taken almost two and a half thousand years for these ideas to be put into practice and for it to have been demonstrated that, despite their bodily differences from men, women can indeed successfully fulfil the social roles which in previous times were exclusively reserved for men. Strauss and Bloom, it seems, do not agree about this, but they do not explain or justify their objections.

More reasoned criticisms of Plato's approach have been voiced by some recent feminists. Women, they maintain, have a distinctive identity, related ultimately to their biology, which would be effaced in Plato's equalitarian meritocracy. Plato's plan is, in effect, to make women into men, into rational Guardians or military Auxiliaries. His proposals involve a denial of the distinctively feminine abilities and virtues. Others dispute this, however. Though Plato does indeed challenge traditional sex roles his purpose is not to force women to be masculine, but rather to allow both women and men to become people who can exercise their natural abilities – whatever these may be – to the full.

All this may make it seem that Plato's philosophy is a form of feminism ahead of its time. Annas disputes this suggestion. Plato is not interested in women's liberation, she argues: he does not care about women's interests or women's rights. 'Plato's proposals are not aimed at relieving the misery and humiliation of women.' His only concern is for the social interest. He sees women as 'a huge untapped pool of resources', which society should use for its good rather than theirs.[5]

---

[4] Strauss, *The City and Man*, pp. 116–17; Bloom, 'Interpretive Essay', pp. 382–3.
[5] Annas, *Introduction to Plato's* Republic, p. 183.

This is quite correct; and it illustrates a general point which is not specific to women. Nothing in the *Republic* is recommended for the sake of one section of the community; all measures are for the social interest, for the good of the whole. This does not mean, however, that Plato's proposals are therefore in any way *contrary* to the interests of women, as Annas at times suggests. Plato clearly believes that it is in women's interests to develop their naturally given abilities and use them to the full, in the service of society. For he rejects the idea which is implied in Annas's criticisms: that there is inevitably a conflict between the interests of the community and those of the individuals or groups which make it up. A harmony of these interests, he believes, is possible.

Marriage and the Family

Plato's ideas about marriage and the family follow directly from his ideas about the role of women. They are even more radical. They provoke a second and even greater 'wave' of sceptical doubt that Plato must answer. If women are to play a full and equal role in the public realm then they must be freed from the demands of managing the household and raising children. Plato proposes that the separate family-household should be abolished among the Guardians. Men and women live together communally, without private homes or private property. Women are 'held in common' in the sense that no woman is the exclusive possession or wife of any individual man. All women are common to all men and vice versa (457c–d).

Sexual relations between men and women are strictly controlled for the good of society. Plato envisages an elaborate system of 'mating festivals' in which the Guardians are paired off by a system of rigged lots. Children born outside these arrangements are treated as illegitimate and perhaps in some cases done away with, though Plato is not very explicit about this.[6]

Children in Plato's republic are reared communally. They do not know their true parents as such, nor do parents know which individual children are their own progeny. Rather, children learn

---

[6] Lee's notes in the Penguin edition, pp. 244–6, give some helpful elucidation on this point as well as further references.

to regard all adults of their parents' generation as their mothers and fathers, and all children of their own generation as brothers and sisters.

Plato's justification for these remarkable proposals is twofold. In the first place, Plato regards the family as a dangerous source of division within the community. His primary concern in abolishing it is to ensure social unity. Second, his motives are eugenic. Both sorts of arguments raise important and controversial issues. I will consider each in turn.

The Need for Social Unity

Plato's conviction that the family poses a potential threat to social unity was undoubtedly justified, particularly at the time he was writing. As with private property – of which the Greeks regarded the family as an extension – the family constitutes a locus for interests and attachments distinct from and potentially in conflict with those of the wider society. Considerations similar to those which lead Plato to abolish private property (see Chapter 5 above) thus apply to the family as well.

In the case of the family, moreover, there are additional factors. When Plato was writing, Athens was only just evolving from being a clan-based society in which the individual's primary loyalty was to the family group. The demands of loyalty to the state (*polis*) were vying for supremacy with ties to family and clan. Conflicts between these two sets of bonds and obligations were real and intense. Such conflicts are the subject of a number of the great tragic dramas of the period. For example, Antigone, in Sophocles' play of that name, is torn between her family duty to honour and bury her brother, Polyneices, and her duty to obey the command of the King, Creon (her uncle), who has ordered Polyneices' body to be left unburied. Her dilemma is tragic and irresolvable. Family ties in this period still exerted a power which threatened allegiance to the state.

Plato's solution is characteristically bold and radical. We are all to regard each other as members of a single great family (*Timaeus* 18c–d). As with the idea of abolishing private property, Plato's aim in abolishing the family is not to do away with family loyalties and family attachments altogether, but rather to transfer them on to the wider community. His purpose is to transfer the bonds which unite the family to the society as a whole. The whole community is to become like one large family in which every member regards all others as family relations.

Aristotle is perhaps the first and still one of the most insightful critics of Plato's plans for the family. He does not reject Plato's ideal of a harmonious and united community; but he does cast doubt on the practicality of Plato's proposals for achieving it. The form of unity of a state is significantly different from that of an individual or a family, he argues: greater diversity is essential to it.[7] Plato's attempt to create social unity by eradicating all private – individual and family – differences would have the opposite effect. Instead of transferring feelings of family concern from the private sphere to the community as a whole, and thus strengthening attachment to the collective, it would weaken these feelings. 'In a state in which wives and children are shared the feelings of affection will inevitably be watery ... Just as a small amount of sweetening dissolved in a large amount of water does not reveal its presence to the taste.'[8]

Many subsequent philosophers have shared Aristotle's scepticism, particularly in relation to modern society. Thus Hegel, in the spirit of Aristotle, maintains that the direct unification of the individual with the community is no longer practical. Modern society has grown too large and complex for this to be possible. Arguably it had already done so by the time Plato was writing, in that it had outgrown its earlier clan-based form. In these conditions a variety of intermediate institutions is needed – such as the family, work and other social arrangements – which can provide smaller and more intimate groupings to which individuals can relate, and through which they can more readily identify with the state and society as a whole.

As usual, Aristotle introduces a salutary note of caution. However, he seems to be assuming that we have only a limited fund of affection which must be divided between those upon whom we bestow it, so that to divide our affections is necessarily to dilute them. But is this the case? Are the attachments in larger families

[7] *Politics* 1261a–b.
[8] *Politics* 1262b.

necessarily less strong than those in smaller ones? If I have four brothers and sisters, do I necessarily regard each with only half the affection I would give to two?

Aristotle's arguments are questionable. Plato's communist ideas about the family, as with his communism about property, are the forerunners of a long and distinguished line of philosophies which have advocated a communal way of life and upbringing of children. Many utopian movements have followed Plato in looking upon all fellow beings as brothers and sisters. Is Aristotle right to reject this on practical grounds? Are universal love and fellowship untenable as human aspirations? Are we not in danger of closing our eyes to our highest possibilities if we rule out any consideration of them on such grounds? These are some of the issues that Plato's philosophy raises.

The Idea of a Planned Society

Of all Plato's ideas, his views on 'marriage' and his proposals for 'mating festivals' regularly provoke the greatest consternation and outrage. The very idea that the most intimate and personal aspects of our lives – love and sexual relations – should be socially planned and regulated seems particularly unacceptable to a modern audience. It is unlikely that it would have provoked such a response among Plato's contemporaries. It is noteworthy that Aristotle does not comment on this issue at all in his detailed discussion of this passage.[9] In ancient Greece, as in many parts of the world up to present times, marriages were arranged. The purpose of marriage was to ensure the satisfactory inheritance of property and to secure political alliances. The idea that it should be a freely chosen relationship based on love and/or sexual attraction is a distinctively modern one, and quite foreign to these societies.

When modern commentators react with horror at the idea of arranged mating and complain that Plato's idea 'does violence to the deepest human emotions',[10] one must remember that marriage was not the locus of the deepest, most intimate relations in ancient

---

[9] *Politics* II.i–v.
[10] Grube, *Plato's Thought*, p. 270; cf. Bloom, 'Interpretive Essay', p. 384; Taylor, *Plato*, p. 278, etc.

Greece. For men at least this was provided by homosexual relations, as Plato makes clear in *The Symposium*. The view that arranged mating for the purposes of reproduction is 'unnatural' and impossible is based upon a very parochial notion of human nature. Although there are natural limits which are determined by our needs both sexual and emotional, these impose only very broad limits on what is humanly possible or satisfactory. The evidence from history and anthropology suggests that there is an enormously diverse range of human possibilities. We should be cautious about trying to rule out arrangements of the sort Plato is suggesting on such grounds, particularly when the arrangements for such matters in our own society are so evidently imperfect.

The idea of controlling reproduction for eugenic purposes arouses an almost equally strong reaction, though for different reasons. Plato propounds his ideas using an analogy with the stockbreeding of animals. His purpose is to breed the 'best' with the 'best' with the aim of rearing a 'pedigree herd' of rulers (459c). To achieve this with human beings, as Plato acknowledges, it will be necessary to employ deceitful means, since people will not consent to being treated in this way. Hence the system of rigged lots which controls who shall mate with whom.

A large part of what is objectionable about all this is the idea that a small and entirely unaccountable elite of Rulers is given such a degree of control over the lives of others, who are regarded simply as 'breeding stock'. However, such unaccountable elitism is a general feature of Plato's political philosophy in the *Republic*, it is not specific to his ideas about the family. (In saying this I am not seeking to endorse this aspect of Plato's philosophy.)

Topical and difficult issues are raised by Plato's view that the state should be involved in family planning for eugenic reasons. He has arguments for this which deserve to be taken seriously. Decisions about reproduction are among the most important we make. Such decisions should be made in a rational and self-conscious fashion, with the social interest in view. 'It would be a sin either for mating or for anything else in a truly happy society to take place without regulation. Our rulers would not allow it' (458d–e).

Eugenic ideas were widely discussed in the earlier years of this century, but their association with Nazism has now made them almost a taboo topic. At the same time, practical developments are putting questions of family planning more and more onto the agenda. The advent of effective contraceptives and their wide availability has meant that people are increasingly exercising a considerable degree of control and planning when it comes to having children, at least as regards numbers and timing.

Plato is more concerned about the quality than the quantity of offspring. This too is coming onto the agenda of modern life. Spectacular advances are being made in medical technology which mean that it will soon be possible to choose the sex and other aspects of the genetic make-up of our children. These developments are opening up eugenic possibilities far beyond anything even dreamed of by Plato. Apprehension about the practical implications of these developments is widespread and well founded. We have every reason to hesitate before we proceed down this path; and we should do so, if at all, only with great caution. The activities of the Nazis stand as a warning of the danger of misusing such techniques and ideas. Moreover, we are now all too well aware that scientific techniques can have unforeseen and unintended consequences, both physical and social.

Much contemporary opposition to genetic engineering is based on the view that to attempt rationally to control and modify fundamental features of biology is in some sense to go 'against nature'. These are modern issues and we have no way of knowing how Plato would have responded to them. Nevertheless, it seems unlikely that he would have taken this view. For Plato rational activity is the very nature of the good. The idea that it is better for non-rational nature to take its course is foreign to his way of thinking.

The new genetic knowledge and techniques give us the possibility of understanding and controlling many aspects of our lives which previously we had to accept as inescapable and unalterable matters of fate. There are good grounds for proceeding with care, but not for closing our eyes and turning our backs on such powers altogether. Self-imposed ignorance has nothing to recommend it. We should act in the light of the fullest available understanding of what is possible and what consequences will follow. This is the spirit of Plato's rationalism. His philosophy embodies the idea of a rationally planned and organised society. This is the main topic of the next section of the dialogue. In this respect,

Plato's philosophy is the forerunner of all subsequent enlightened and critical social philosophies.

Guide to Further Reading

This section raises issues which have been central to a great deal of modern social and political debate. It has generated a huge literature in recent times. There is a good general account in Annas, *Introduction to Plato's* Republic, Chapter 7; see also Barker's earlier but still useful discussion in *Greek Political Theory*, Chapter 10. For more on the position of women in ancient Greece, see K. J. Dover, *Greek Homosexuality*, and H. D. F. Kitto, *The Greeks*, Chapter 12.

The view that Plato's proposals for women and the family are meant ironically is developed by Strauss, *The City and Man*, Chapter 2, and in Bloom, 'Interpretive Essay'. For criticisms of this view, see D. Hall, 'The *Republic* and the "Limits of Politics"', S. M. Okin, 'Philosopher Queens and Private Wives: Plato on Women and the Family', and C. Pierce, 'Equality: *Republic* V'.

The view that Plato ignores the differences between women and men is developed in different ways by D. H. Coole, *Women in Political Theory*, Chapter 2, and J. B. Elshtain, *Public Man, Private Woman*, Chapter 1, and well criticised by Okin in the article just cited.

Plato's views on the family are criticised in Aristotle, *Politics* II.i–v. There is little recent literature on Plato's eugenic ideas, but see J. J. Mulhern, 'Population and Plato's *Republic*' and W. Fortenbaugh, 'Plato, Temperament and Eugenic Policy'. S. Jones, *The Language of the Genes*, gives a useful overview of recent advances in genetics and discusses their practical implications in clear and accessible terms.

9 Philosophy and Society
(V.471c–VI.502c)

The passages from Books V–VII (471c–541b) which are the sub-ject of the next three chapters deal with the nature of philosophical knowledge and the training needed to develop it. They stand out from the rest of the dialogue in that they focus on issues in epis-temology, metaphysics and logic, and introduce Plato's Theory of Forms.

At first these topics seem remote from the moral and social issues with which the *Republic* is primarily concerned. They appear to be a digression – indeed, a digression within a digression – from the main argument of the dialogue. This is not the case, however. Moral and social philosophy is not a self-contained field cut off from other areas of thought. Ideas about the individual and society inevitably involve presuppositions about the nature of reality and our knowledge of it.

In particular, the Theory of Forms plays an essential role in the main argument of the *Republic*. Plato's account of justice cannot be completed without it. As Plato has earlier said, the description of justice as a sort of harmony is 'incomplete', only a 'sketch' (504d), it is superficial and approximate. The Theory of Forms is required in order to complete it. Moreover, the just society, for Plato, is under the control of Guardians who rule by virtue of their knowledge. Plato describes this knowledge as 'philoso-phy'. What is the nature of this knowledge, and what sort of education is needed to develop it? These are the questions that Plato now tackles. It is in this context that he needs the Theory of Forms.

The Utopian Approach

In the dialogue Socrates is led to these issues through his attempt to answer what he calls the third and greatest 'wave' of sceptical doubt which his views must overcome. This involves a question which will surely have occurred to many readers of the *Republic*. Even if we accept the picture of the just society that Plato has been describing, it will be said, it is only a theoretical construction, only an ideal. Though such a society may seem attractive in theory, that goes no way to showing that it could actually exist in practice (471c–472e). Plato takes this as an objection, not just to the specific ideas of the *Republic*, but to its utopian approach. He takes it to be expressing the view that there is no point in speculating and dreaming about an ideal society. It is better to be realistic and practical, and keep one's sights firmly focused on the actual world, no matter how unsatisfactory and unideal it may be.

Plato's response is bold and vigorous. In the strongest terms he defends the value of the utopian approach which is such a striking feature of the *Republic*. The society he has been describing, he admits, is indeed an ideal. It does not exist in reality, nor could it possibly do so. For the ideal society is a quite different sort of thing than any actually existing society. The ideal society is perfect, whereas all actual societies are, in various ways, imperfect. Moreover, there is only one social ideal which remains constant, while there are many different actual societies which are changing continually. Thus the ideal is not and cannot be actual.

'A map of the world that does not include Utopia is not worth even glancing at', says Oscar Wilde with characteristic wit and brilliance.[1] The ideal society is not the sort of thing that can appear on any map; it is not located in space and time. But that does not mean that it is a useless illusion or dream. On the contrary. Like a map, the ideal provides a standard, a 'pattern' (*paradeigma*), by which existing societies can be judged and criticised. The ideal also serves as a guide to action by showing us the end towards which we should aim, even though we can never finally reach it (472c). However, for Plato the ideal is a truer sort of reality than that depicted on any map and it is the object of genuine knowledge. In this it resembles the Forms.

[1] O. Wilde, 'The Soul of Man under Socialism', p. 34.

The Forms are like the ideal also in that they cannot be encountered through the senses but are known only to thought. Our knowledge of them is given by what Plato calls 'philosophy'. This is the knowledge that must be possessed by the rulers of the ideal society. Thus Plato is led to propound what he regards as the greatest paradox he defends in the dialogue.

> The society we have described can never grow into a reality or see the light of day . . . till philosophers become kings in this world, or till those we now call kings and rulers really and truly become philosophers, and political power and philosophy thus come into the same hands . . . there is no other road to real happiness, either for society or the individual.[2]

The paradox in this may be somewhat mitigated for the modern reader by realising that by 'philosophy' here Plato means something much broader than its modern meaning suggests. He is delineating the subject for the first time. He was writing long before philosophy had developed into a specialised academic subject separate from the natural and social sciences or from other disciplines in the humanities. Philosophy, as he conceives of it, covers all these fields. It includes mathematics and geometry, the various branches of the natural sciences and history. It encompasses rational knowledge of all kinds. Plato distinguishes it mainly by contrast with, on the one hand, poetry (itself a broad term in Plato, covering all forms of imaginative literature including drama, fable, etc.), and, on the other hand, rhetoric, that is, non-rational forms of persuasion. By a society ruled by philosophy, therefore, what Plato is proposing is a rationally directed society.

The Nature of Philosophical Knowledge

To explain the nature of philosophy Plato appeals initially to the root meaning of the word. Philosophy is the love of knowledge. It is, for Plato, the love of all knowledge, the desire for comprehensive and universal understanding. Glaucon now asks how the philosopher differs from the dilettante whose omnivorous curiosity leads to a desire for every possible sensation and experience (the 'sight-lover' (476b)). This prompts Plato to introduce the Theory of Forms.

[2] *Republic* 473c–e.

This theory deals with some fundamental metaphysical issues and will be discussed more fully in the next chapter. For the present I will focus on Plato's attempt to defend the idea of philosophical rule and the moral and political issues raised by this. The term 'Form' is a translation of the Greek *idea*. Many earlier commentators talk of Plato's 'Theory of Ideas'. Modern translators have tended to prefer the term 'Form'. This avoids giving the impression of something in the mind and subjective. A Form, according to Plato, is a rational ordering of things which is not merely subjective, but rather objective and a part of the fabric of things themselves.

To explain the notion of a Form in Book V Plato focuses particularly on the concepts of justice, beauty and goodness.[3] There are many things that we encounter in the course of experience which have these qualities in varying degrees. Plato calls such particular, just, beautiful or good things 'sensible' objects because we are acquainted with them through the senses. Apart from this multiplicity of particular things which are more or less just, beautiful or good, however, we must distinguish Justice, Beauty and Goodness 'themselves' or 'as such'. These are Forms. Like the ideal society, they are not encountered through experience; they can be known only in thought, by the use of reason. They are 'intelligible' objects.

Thus Plato believes that there are two orders of reality, 'two worlds': the sensible realm made up of the objects of everyday experience and the intelligible realm of the Forms (see Chapter 10 for further discussion). According to Plato, the realm of eternal and unchanging Forms is the fullest and highest reality. It and it alone is the object of genuine knowledge. Our apprehension of sensible phenomena is called *doxa* – 'belief' or 'opinion' (Lee's preferred translation) – by Plato. It is in these terms that Plato now distinguishes true philosophy, which involves a knowledge of Forms, from dilettante curiosity – love of belief or 'philodoxy' as Plato now terms it (480a).

Most people's consciousness never reaches beyond the level of such beliefs about the transitory and fluctuating world of the

---

[3] This leaves unresolved the question of whether or not there is a Form for *every* universal term.

senses. Plato compares this level of awareness with the dim and
deluded experience of dreams. Genuine knowledge, by contrast, is
like full waking consciousness. Only the philosopher, by the use of
reason, can achieve it. This contrast is most graphically depicted in
the allegory of the cave. The dark condition of ordinary consciousness is represented by the prisoners seeing shadows in the cave,
while the enlightenment which comes from philosophical knowledge is portrayed by the image of sunlight.

The Philosopher in Society

It may seem that we have moved far away from the central
concerns of the *Republic*, but this is not so. In the first place, with
the Theory of Forms, Plato aims to establish that there is an
objective basis for his account of justice and for the political and
moral ideas which flow from it. The ideal of justice that he has
been advocating is not merely his own subjective opinion, nor is it
simply a matter of social convention, as Glaucon and Adeimantus
suggest. The ideal of justice has objective existence: it is a Form.

Philosophical knowledge is necessary to grasp this Form: that is,
to know the principles which determine the nature of justice rather
than merely some of the instances of it. Non philosophers, such as
Cephalus and Polemarchus at the beginning of the dialogue, have
some grasp of instances of justice. However, the conceptions of
justice with which they operate – such as repaying debts, and
giving each person their due – are mere rules of thumb. That is not
to say that they are baseless principles, but their truth is limited.
They are generalisations based on experience, satisfactory as far as
they go: but their application is limited, as Socrates demonstrates
in Book I. They fall short of genuine knowledge of the Form or
principle of justice, which gives the essential nature of justice and
applies universally, in every case.

In this way, Plato maintains that there is a real difference
between justice and injustice which exists quite independently
of people's beliefs and opinions. Moreover, there is real knowledge, real expertise, involved in knowing this difference, which
some people have and others lack. Plato thus attempts to vindicate
his analogy of the philosophically enlightened ruler with a doctor
or navigator.

The philosophical ruler has a clear 'vision' of a 'standard of perfection' (*paradeigma*) by which to guide society. Whereas the ruler without such knowledge is like a 'blind' person (484c). Moreover, repeating a point he has already made on the basis of his theory of the self (444a–e), Plato goes on to argue at length that the philosopher's pleasures are mental rather than physical. Philosophers are less likely to be attracted by the desires and appetites. Consequently they are more likely to develop the other main virtues of self-discipline and courage as well as wisdom. The philosopher is the person best qualified to rule (485d–487a).

At this point Adeimantus makes an important objection. No matter how good the idea of rule by philosophers may sound in theory, he says, it would not work in practice. All experience tells us that philosophers are not the sort of people who are cut out to be rulers: most of them are useless, while a few of them are positively vicious and dangerous. Plato answers this objection in a powerful and passionate passage which in all probability reflects his own experience (487b–497a). There are two prongs to his response.

First, and no doubt with the fate of Socrates in mind, he argues that if a society has no use for the genuine philosopher, it is not philosophy which is at fault, but rather the society which has no understanding of it nor any use for it. He compares a corrupt society (which is how he sees the Athens of his time) with a ship. The captain is well meaning but weak. He is a little deaf and short-sighted, and not a competent seaman. The crew are constantly quarrelling about how to navigate the ship, though none of them has learned the science of navigation. Indeed none believes in the existence of such a science, though each one thinks that he alone should be in charge of the ship and tries to influence the captain accordingly.

There is also a true navigator on board, who maintains that to steer the right course one must study the stars. The crew scoff at this and dismiss him as a useless dreamer. Nevertheless, Plato says, the navigator is not useless. It is rather the crew and the captain who, in their ignorance and blindness, have no use for such a person (487b–489c). In other words, true philosophy is not socially useless; the fault lies rather with an ignorant society which has no use for it.

What should the true philosopher do in this situation? Contrary to what some of his critics suggest, Plato does not advocate mere conformity. On the contrary, he believes that one should fight corrupt conditions in so far as one can. If this is not possible, however, rather than joining in 'the general wickedness', one would be wiser 'to live quietly and keep to [oneself], like a man who stands under the shelter of a wall during a driving storm' (496d).[4]

As to the charge that some philosophers are positively vicious, Plato maintains that most of those claiming to be philosophers are frauds and charlatans. In so far as those born with genuine philosophical ability are dangerous that is because they have been corrupted by society. So again, though the charge that philosophy is harmful may sometimes have a basis, the fault lies not with philosophy but rather with the evil influence of society.

In most of the other dialogues it is the Sophists who are the main targets of criticism and who are held responsible for perverting philosophy and bringing it into disrepute. Here, however, Plato suggests that the impact of such teachers is secondary by comparison with the force of public opinion. It is the public which is the 'great Sophist' (492a–b). In another vivid and powerful analogy Plato compares the public with a large and powerful beast whose needs and wants must be placated, whatever they may be. Public opinion is similarly demanding, but shallow and superficial. It will never accept the idea of an intelligible world of Forms or appreciate true philosophy. Those who are born with genuine philosophical ability will be coopted and corrupted; at the same time charlatans and frauds will claim to be philosophers. What should be an honourable title is thus discredited. Only the exceptional individual, by some accident, can succeed in escaping these destructive influences and grow into a true philosopher. And then, seeing the general corruption all around, such a person will prefer to keep himself to himself.

Things would be different in a better society, in which true philosophers could develop and use their talents fully, for the good of the community and for their own good (497a). There is nothing

---

[4] *Letter* VII suggests that this was the attitude adopted by Plato himself in his own life.

impossible in this, Plato insists: there is no inherent impossibility in the idea of a society ruled philosophically. And perhaps, some set of circumstances may compel the minority of uncorrupted philosophers now treated as useless to participate in politics and make society listen to them (499b). It is in these terms that Plato answers the third wave of doubts and vindicates the idea of philosophical rule.

The Idea of a Rational Society

Stripped of its individual form, Plato's proposal for philosopher-rulers embodies the idea of a rationally planned and directed society. This is one of the most fundamental and important ideas in the whole history of western political thought. Society need not be a product of haphazard and unconscious customs and traditions. Its main forms and structures, together with the forces governing their development, can be understood in rational terms, and planned and organised so as to meet human needs and increase human well-being. This has been the aspiration of enlightened politics through the ages.

Plato's philosophy is noteworthy for the thoroughgoing consistency with which he develops this vision. His radicalism is breathtaking. Nothing is to be preserved merely because it has 'always been like that'. All social structures and beliefs are to be examined and, if necessary, transformed to bring them into accord with the demands of reason.

This rational approach to social thought has been the model for radical and utopian political projects ever since. A similar belief in the possibility of radically transforming society for the human good according to rational and scientific principles is the inspiration for the French Revolution in the eighteenth century, and for subsequent revolutionary movements down to the present-day.

Critics, however, often see this approach as the source of all that is dangerous in Plato's political philosophy. They attack what they see as Plato's excessive rationalism, his faith in reason alone to guide the construction of a new world, and the radicalism to which it gives rise. Barker, for example, charges that Plato 'starts from absolute principles, and arrives at equally absolute conclusions', and that he thus institutes a 'tyranny of reason'.

Barker justifies these charges with a common argument. 'In the realm of man's action there is and there must be an absence of utter logic.'[5] Plato is aware that there are other forces besides reason at work in human life. Nevertheless, he believes that they can be brought under the harmonious control of reason. This is what Barker is disputing. Whether he is right is not clear. It is true that our understanding of human action is far from complete. Just for this reason, however, we are not in a position to say whether what presently seems illogical in it results from an 'absence of logic' or whether it is due to the limitations of our knowledge.

The classic expression of the conservative case is put by the eighteenth-century writer Edmund Burke.[6] Society is not a rational construction. Rather it is like a delicate organism which we tamper with at our peril. Popper gives a modern version of the conservative position. He seeks to set limits to the role of reason in politics which exclude any projects of radical social change as such. He attacks as 'utopian' all attempts to 'realize an ideal state, using a blueprint of society as a whole'. In contrast to Plato he wants to confine the role of reason in social life within the parameters of the existing order. Rationally planned social change should be restricted to 'piecemeal social engineering', to gradual, small-scale reforms.[7]

His reason is that only small-scale changes can be predicted with any certainty. The impact of large-scale policies is too diffuse to be the subject of prediction or rational assessment. This is true. However, large-scale policies are unavoidable in the political process. Popper appears to imagine that maintaining the *status quo* and effecting only 'piecemeal' changes avoids the problem. It does not. What he is recommending is in effect a large-scale policy of conservatism, of resistance to radical change.

No doubt, as Popper argues, the effects of attempting to change society radically are impossible to assess with precision. The revolutionary project is fraught with danger and can cause great suffering; but so too can conservative resistance to change when it means perpetuating great wrong and injustice. There are no valid

---

[5] Barker, *Political Thought of Plato and Aristotle*, p. 162.
[6] Burke, *Reflections on the Revolution in France*.
[7] *The Open Society*, Vol. I, p. 159. Cf. Popper, *The Poverty of Historicism*, Sect. 21.

grounds which show a priori that piecemeal reform is necessarily and in all circumstances preferable to radical change. On the contrary, as Carr says,

> Progress in human affairs, whether in science or in history or in society, has come mainly through the bold readiness of human beings not to confine themselves to seeking piecemeal improvements in the way things are done, but to present fundamental challenges in the name of reason to the current way of doing things, and to the avowed or hidden assumptions on which it rests.[8]

The Idea of Philosophical Rule

For Plato, philosophical rule implies an aristocratic form of government and the rejection of democracy. Only an elite few, he believes, have the ability to acquire a knowledge of philosophy.[9] The democratic principle that the ordinary people should have a role in ruling society is, for Plato, a recipe for rule by the ignorant and incompetent. It means handing control over to the whims of the 'great and powerful beast' of public opinion.

This criticism of democracy should not be too hastily dismissed; there is surely some truth to it. Even if we reject Plato's view that the mass of the people can never achieve true knowledge, it remains true that public opinion is shallow and ill-informed and easily swayed by demagogues. Popular sovereignty is probably not the best way to achieve wisdom in government. However, it has other virtues.

In the ideal world of Plato's republic, where rulers really do have knowledge of the good and always use it in the social interest, one of the important reasons for democracy would be absent. The Guardians can be trusted with their power. Things are different in the real, imperfect world. Where interests conflict and rulers are fallible, giving unchecked power to those claiming to be 'experts' is a recipe for tyranny.

The first priority in an imperfect world is to ensure that those with political power do not use it merely to further their own

[8] E. H. Carr, *What is History?* p. 155.

[9] There is a natural hierarchy, according to Plato: some are born to rule, others to be ruled. 'The ignorant should follow the leadership of the wise', as Plato expresses the fundamental principle of his political philosophy in the *Laws* (690d).

interests, but heed the interests of those they rule. An important function of the democratic control of government is to ensure that it is responsive to the interests of the people. Plato is oblivious to this concern, and for this he must be criticised.

Is Plato 'Anti-political'?

Plato is sometimes accused of being an 'anti-political' philosopher. This sounds paradoxical: Plato says a great deal about the way society should be governed. However, he says nothing about the political mechanisms through which fundamental disagreements and clashes of interests can be resolved. His account of the ideal society focuses exclusively on the notion of a harmonious community. It contains no means for handling conflict. For this reason, Plato's philosophy is criticised for envisaging an impossible world from which politics has been banished.

Strauss takes this line of argument even further. The society described in the *Republic* is so unreal, he maintains, that it is a mistake to interpret it as a utopian ideal at all. Rather, it is an ironic picture of an absurd and unrealisable situation, intended to discredit the very idea of philosophical politics. The *Republic*, he says, represents 'the broadest and deepest analysis of political idealism ever made'.[10]

As an interpretation of the *Republic* this is absurd and untenable. Plato is perfectly well aware of the existence of conflict in the actual world, and of the need for mechanisms to deal with it. He puts forward the notion of a harmonious community ruled by rational principles explicitly as an ideal. If politics is supposed to exist only where there is social conflict, then Plato's aim is indeed the abolition of politics. By the same token, the modern communist ideal of a classless society is 'anti-political'. Plato was the first in a long line of political philosophers who have put forward this ideal. There are no good grounds for believing that his intentions are in any way ironic. What those who describe Plato's philosophy as 'anti-political' mean is that his vision of social harmony is unattainable. That is a tenable view, but there are no good grounds for attributing it to Plato.

---

[10] Strauss, *The City and Man*, p. 127.

Berlin is making a similar criticism of Plato's approach when he writes,

> One belief, more than any other, is responsible for the slaughter of individuals on the altars of great historical ideas ... This is the belief that somewhere, in the past or in the future ... in the pronouncements of history or science ... there is a final solution. This ancient faith rests on the conviction that all the positive values in which men have believed must, in the end, be compatible, and perhaps even entail one another.[11]

In part, this is an attempt to smear Plato (together with Marx and Hegel) by association with Nazism – a technique of argument which has, unfortunately, been much used by Plato's liberal critics, but which is none the less disreputable for that. As Versenyi rightly observes, it is quite wrong to equate Plato's republic with modern totalitarianism.

> No man argued more consistently and with greater insight against despotism than Plato. His authoritarianism was aristocratic, not despotic ... One simply cannot point to the most unenlightened and irrational absolute rulers in history and use them as arguments against Plato's principle that the best man, the man with greatest knowledge of the good, should rule.[12]

However, Berlin is also making a more substantial point. He rejects the Platonic vision of a harmonious society in which the Rulers act as guardians of the common interest. 'The notion of a final harmony', he asserts, is a 'metaphysical chimera'. Like the Sophists, he maintains that in the real world people's interests inevitably conflict and cannot be harmonised.

Plato can be criticised for focusing too much on the ideal and paying too little attention to the problems of the real world; but he knows perfectly well that peoples' ends often in fact conflict. What he rejects is Berlin's pessimistic picture of human nature – his bleak view that social conflict is inevitable, and that all we can hope for is a more or less satisfactory compromise between incompatible interests. The main purpose of his philosophy is not to describe the actual world and its problems, but to offer a vision of an ideal to strive towards.

[11] Berlin, 'Two Concepts of Liberty', p. 167.
[12] L. G. Versenyi, 'Plato and His Liberal Opponents', p. 231.

Guide to Further Reading

The literature on Plato's Theory of Forms is vast. Much of it concerns the epistemological, metaphysical and logical aspects which I focus on in the next chapter. Here I shall concentrate on general works and on material dealing with the moral and social aspects of this passage.

As to general accounts, Nettleship, *Lectures*, Chapters 9–12, gives an excellent introductory survey of these sections of the *Republic*. His interpretation particularly stresses the religious dimension of Plato's thought. Annas, *Introduction to Plato's Republic*, Chapters 8–11, also contains a good introductory account focused more on logical issues. Cross and Woozley, *Plato's Republic*, Chapters 7–8, is also useful although dated at times.

Grube, *Plato's Thought*, Chapter 1, has a brief summary of the treatment of the Theory of Forms throughout Plato's work. A more detailed account can be found in I. M. Crombie, *An Examination of Plato's Doctrines*. Volume I contains a useful brief account of the moral and political uses of the Theory of Forms, while Volume II has a detailed discussion of its metaphysical and logical aspects.

On the political implications of Plato's rationalism, see Barker, *Greek Political Theory*, Chapter 11. Popper's influential criticisms of Plato's politics are in his *The Open Society*, Volume I, Chapter 9. Articles discussing Popper's views are usefully collected in Bambrough (ed.), *Plato, Popper and Politics*.

The view that Plato is 'anti-political' is presented by W. A. R. Leys, 'Was Plato Non-Political?' Strauss's interpretation of Plato as an ironist is set out in *The City and Man*, Chapter 2, and trenchantly criticised in Hall, 'The *Republic* and the "Limits of Politics"'.

10　The Theory of Forms

The Theory of Forms raises so many philosophical issues that it requires a chapter to itself. Its central tenet, as we have briefly seen, is that there is a realm of entities not present to the senses and accessible only by reason. These entities – the Forms – are the truest reality and the objects of genuine knowledge.

These ideas will be strange and unfamiliar to many readers. Philosophy in the English-speaking world has long been dominated by a very different, empiricist philosophy. According to this, the world given to the senses is the only reality, and the senses are the source of all our knowledge. However, the Platonic approach has much to recommend it. It has been fundamental to philosophy in the rationalist tradition which has been particularly influential in continental Europe.

Some Examples

Perhaps the most familiar examples of intelligible objects come from mathematics and geometry. For Plato these subjects are paradigms of knowledge and serve to introduce the Forms.

Mathematics deals with abstract entities not knowable through the senses. Experience can acquaint us with groups of particular objects: two apples, three oranges, and so forth. Such objects and the way they are grouped alter and change. Numbers themselves, by contrast, cannot be seen or touched or otherwise encountered in experience. Numbers and truths about them (e.g., '$2 + 2 = 4$') constitute an eternal and unchanging world knowable only by thought.

Similarly, geometry deals with intelligible and not sensible objects. The actual triangular or rectangular shapes that we encounter through the senses are imperfect, irregular and changing. They only approximate to the figures dealt with in geometry. For geometry concerns a realm of purely theoretical entities: figures constructed on a perfectly plain surface out of absolutely uniform lines of zero thickness which are eternal and unchanging and knowable only through thought (510c–d).

The study of mathematics puts us in touch with the intelligible world. It helps to detach the mind from senses and lead it to abstract thought. For this reason, Plato recommends that the higher education of the Guardians should begin with arithmetic and geometry as a path leading to the world of the Forms.

According to Plato, however, all genuine knowledge of the world has a rational character. For this reason, his programme of higher education also includes astronomy: not for its practical benefits, but because it too helps to train the mind to think abstractly. To the senses, the planets appear now here, now there. But behind this mass of changing observations science looks for a rational order: it seeks for unchanging universal laws. These can be grasped only by thought. In Hegel's words, 'the laws of the celestial motions are not written on the sky. The universal is neither seen nor heard, its existence is only for the mind.'[1]

Indeed, the ability to distinguish different kinds and species, which is fundamental to all knowledge, is ultimately the work of reason. Again Hegel puts it well. 'Individuals are born and perish: the species abides and recurs in them all: and its existence is visible only to reflection'.[2]

The Two 'Worlds'

I have cited these examples in order to explain the idea of an intelligible realm in contrast to the world given to the senses. Similar examples are used in the scheme of higher education which Plato describes in Book VII. In the main account of the Theory of

[1] G. W. F. Hegel, *Logic*, p. 43.
[2] Ibid., p. 42.

Forms, however, Plato focuses on beauty, justice and goodness. A similar contrast holds in these cases. Through experience we encounter many particular things which are more or less beautiful, just or good; but we must distinguish from these the Forms of Beauty, Justice or the Good themselves. These Forms are known only by thought.

Thus, according to Plato, there are two orders of reality, two 'worlds': a sensible world given to experience and an intelligible world of Forms, accessible only through thought. The objects of these two worlds have quite opposite properties. There are many particular things which are to some extent beautiful. The Form – Beauty itself – by contrast is one and single. The many particular beautiful things are variously described as 'instances' of the Form: they are said to 'share' or 'participate' in it or, alternatively, to 'copy' or 'resemble' it.

Sensible objects are imperfect. No particular beautiful thing is absolutely beautiful. In some respect it will be imperfect, in some respect it will be ugly. It may appear beautiful to me, but ugly to you. Moreover, particular beautiful things exist in space and time and are subject to change and decay. They will eventually cease to be beautiful and become ugly. Indeed, in time all particular things will pass away and cease to exist altogether. The Form of Beauty, by contrast, is perfect: it is eternal and unchanging. It excludes its opposite, ugliness; it is unqualifiedly beautiful.

The eternal Forms are the fullest and highest reality. These, and these alone, are the objects of genuine knowledge. The objects given to the senses are fleeting and transient particulars. The consciousness of most people, according to Plato, never reaches beyond these. It involves only 'belief' or 'opinion' (*doxa*). Genuine knowledge (*epistēmē* or *noēsis*) is quite different. It is based upon the use of reason and engages with the world of the Forms. Only a few have the rational ability to attain it.

The Objects of Belief and Knowledge

In the dialogue, the notion of the Forms is introduced by Socrates as though it was already familiar to the other participants (475e). Then it is explained and defended for the uninitiated with a lengthy and elaborate argument. This revolves around the difference between belief and knowledge which are distinguished by their objects (476e–480a). Plato maintains that belief occupies an intermediate position between true knowledge and total ignorance (by which Plato seems to mean something like delusion). The object of knowledge is what is fully real, what truly is. Ignorance or delusion concerns what is unreal and has no existence. Belief lies between these extremes. Its object is contradictory: it both is and is not.

What does Plato mean by this? Many recent commentators have tried to elucidate Plato's position in purely logical terms. The Forms have their characteristics in an unqualified way, whereas sensible particulars have the properties they have only with qualifications. The Form of F is unqualifiedly F, while a sensible object is an F only in specific conditions: at a particular time, or from a particular perspective, or whatever.[3]

There is also a metaphysical and epistemological aspect to Plato's theory, embodied in the views that I have just been explaining. Sensible objects constitute a lesser order of reality in the sense that they are imperfect, changeable and transient, whereas the Forms are perfect, eternal and unchanging. Moreover, because they are imperfect and transitory, the particular things encountered in experience are never absolutely and unchangingly what they are. They are always afflicted with their opposites. A particular beautiful thing is always in some respects also ugly, and its beauty is destined to fade. In this sense, such a thing – and not just the predicates that can be used to describe it – is contradictory.

The notion that there are different degrees of reality sounds strange to modern ears: we tend to regard things as either real or not. Stranger still is the suggestion that the intelligible realm of the Forms – a world accessible only to thought – is more real than the world of familiar objects which we can see and touch. For philosophy in the English-speaking world has long been dominated by the empiricist view that the world given to the senses is the only reality. Plato rejects such empiricism, and he has good reasons to do so. As I have been arguing, there is much in our knowledge which is not given to the senses. There are entities like numbers, and there is a deeper and more fundamental – rational

---

[3] Vlastos, 'Degrees of Reality in Plato'; N. P. White, *A Companion to Plato's* Republic, pp. 30–43.

and law-like – order of things which is not revealed outwardly to the senses but which can be known only by thought.

It is easy to read into this the view that the world given to the senses is illusory. At times this is what Plato himself seems to imply. It is therefore important to see that in this passage at least Plato explicitly rejects this view. In maintaining that the objects of belief are midway between those of knowledge and ignorance, he is denying that they are entirely unreal. Likewise, when he says that sensible objects are contradictory, he must not be taken to mean that they are unreal, but rather that they are changeable and transitory. I shall return to this issue in a moment.

Plato's account of the Forms can also be read epistemologically. Here too his views seem strange to modern ears. Since Descartes philosophers have tended to distinguish knowledge from belief primarily in terms of its certainty and immunity from sceptical doubt. Plato makes a similar distinction. Genuine knowledge, he says, is 'infallible' (477e). If I know something then I cannot be mistaken about it, whereas beliefs are fallible. However, this is not what primarily distinguishes them for Plato. Knowledge and belief, he maintains, result from different faculties – reason and the senses (477d–e) – and they have different objects – reality and appearances (477b). These views are not part of the usual modern notions of knowledge and belief.

For Plato knowledge is not just a matter of certainty. It involves a direct acquaintance with a truer reality which results in full and genuine understanding. Plato compares it to waking consciousness. Conversely, the condition of belief is not just one of doubt, it is one of illusion. Plato likens it to dreaming. In it, we are acquainted with 'images', 'shadows' or appearances which we mistake for reality. Sensory appearances are deceptive. We must detach ourselves from them and from reliance on the senses if we are to achieve true knowledge. We must grasp a different – a higher and truer – order of reality which is accessible only to rational thought.[4]

---

[4] There is a particularly strong statement of this theme in *Phaedo* 65b–67b. In his *Meditations*, Descartes also insists that we must detach ourselves from the senses and use reason if we are to achieve genuine knowledge. For an account of this theme in modern philosophy, see S. Sayers, *Reality and Reason*, Ch. 2.

Again, it must be stressed that Plato is not suggesting that sensory appearances are purely illusory. On the contrary, this is explicitly rejected by Plato in this passage when he maintains that the objects of the senses occupy an intermediate grade of being. Though on the one hand the reality of the Forms is not given immediately in sensory appearances, on the other hand it is not entirely absent from them either. In other words, reality in the shape of the Forms is present to the senses through appearances, although in only an imperfect way.

The Problem of Dualism

Elsewhere, however, Plato seems to denigrate the senses and their objects altogether. Often he seems to suggest that the intelligible realm is the sole reality, quite separate from and independent of the false and illusory world given to the senses. Dualistic talk of two 'worlds' runs throughout his work. It is one of its most character-istic and distinctive features.[5] Many of the problems associated with the Theory of Forms stem from this.

Such dualism is particularly evident in the account of the Forms given in the *Phaedo*. In the *Republic* it is most apparent in the allegory of the cave (514a–521b) where there seems to be no connection between the dark world of the senses down in the cave and the sunlit realm of rational knowledge above. Philoso-phical knowledge, on this view, seems to involve the contemplation of a higher realm, quite separate from the obscure and imperfect world of the senses.

These views cannot be squared with other things that Plato says. Elsewhere he portrays sensible objects as 'images' or 'representa-tions' of the Forms, and thus implies that there is an essential relation between them. As we have just seen, this is the point that Plato is making when he describes sensible objects as midway between the full reality of the Forms and the complete non-being of delusion. Moreover, Plato insists that the Guardians need a knowledge of the Forms in order to rule society well. Once they

---

[5] According to Aristotle, Socrates did not conceive of Forms apart from their instances; this was an innovation of Plato and/or his followers (*Metaphysics* 1078b–1079a, cf. 987a–b).

have attained it, they must leave the sunlight and return to the cave to put their knowledge of the Forms to use. It cannot therefore consist only in the contemplation of another world, it must give an understanding which is relevant and useful in this world.

These conflicting views suggest that Plato was genuinely uncertain on this issue. Those who focus on Plato's talk of two 'worlds' tend to reject the Theory of Forms as an unworkable dualism which suggests that lurking somehow beyond or behind the things given to the senses there is another and more real world of Forms.

What is illuminating in Plato's philosophy cannot be understood in these terms. However, a different and more viable interpretation is possible, even if it is not always the one explicitly given by Plato. This conceives of the Forms as the reality of things, whereas the sensible realm is the way in which *this same reality* appears to a more superficial view which relies on the senses. There are not two separate 'worlds' or order of things involved here. Rather there are two different ways in which things can appear to us, two different aspects that a thing can present to us.[6]

In short there is only one world. To the senses it presents only a superficial and fleeting series of appearances. Rational thought is needed to grasp its real nature. This is the view standardly adopted in the sciences, where the unchanging order of laws and forces described by scientific theory is regarded as giving a truer and better picture of the real nature of things than is revealed to immediate observation.

A Priori Knowledge

The view that we know of the Forms through reason rather than via the senses implies that we have knowledge independently of and prior to any experience: 'a priori' knowledge as it is called in modern philosophy. This point is not given much attention in the *Republic*, but it is an essential part of the epistemology of the Theory of Forms and more fully discussed elsewhere by Plato.

Empiricist philosophy denies the very possibility of a priori knowledge. At birth, it holds, the mind is blank: all our knowledge

[6] An account along these lines is given by Heidegger, *Nietzsche*, Vol. I, Chs 21–2.

of the world comes to us through experience. Plato argues against this view in very striking terms in the *Meno*. By questioning a young, uneducated slave boy, who has no previous knowledge of geometry, Socrates gets him to carry out a geometric proof. Socrates insists, quite plausibly, that he has not provided the boy with the answers. He has merely elicited knowledge which was in the boy's mind already even though he was not aware that he possessed it.

Where, then, does such knowledge come from? To answer this question Plato recounts a myth. As always, when he appeals to myth in this way he is not putting it forward as mere fable or fantasy, but rather as an expression of ideas which he believes to be true but for which he lacks proof.[7]

Poets, sages and others who are 'divinely inspired' believe, so Plato says, that the soul is immortal (*Meno* 81b). It does not perish with the death of the body. It migrates elsewhere and is eventually reborn in another body. Through many reincarnations it accumulates a knowledge of all that is. We do not consciously realise we have this knowledge but it is latent in all of us. It is recollected when something in our present awareness reawakens it. Thus 'seeking and learning are in fact nothing but recollection' (ibid., 81d). A priori truths, such as those of mathematics and geometry, do not need to be taught. A knowledge of them is already innate in us, waiting to be recollected from a previous life. The philosopher is merely a 'midwife' helping to bring to consciousness what is already implicitly present in the mind (*Theaetetus* 149a–151d).

In this way, Plato expresses ideas that have played a fundamental role in rationalist accounts of knowledge ever since. Thinkers from Descartes and Leibniz in the seventeenth century through to contemporaries such as Chomsky have maintained that there are 'innate ideas'. By this they do not mean – as Plato's recollection theory seems to suggest – that we are born with a knowledge of geometry and other such matters already present within us. There are no grounds to believe that geometry is actually inscribed in the infant mind. However, when it is developed the mind does possess the ability to generate these ideas a

---

[7] It is in this spirit that he presents the Myth of Er about the immortality of the soul in Book X (see Ch. 14 below).

priori, not on the basis of experience but through the use of its rational powers alone.[8]

Forms as Essences

In Aristotle's words, the Theory of Forms embodies the idea of 'one over many'. Its central thought is that common to the many particular instances of justice, for example, but distinct from them, there is a single Form, Justice itself, by virtue of which the instances are instances of justice. If one and the same term is used correctly to described a number of different instances, there must be some characteristic that they share in common (*Meno* 72c–d).

Plato was led to this theory, Aristotle tells us, by the Socratic search for definitions which is portrayed in many of the dialogues. To determine the nature of justice we must discover its defining characteristic, its essence. We must determine the common feature that all cases of justice share and that makes them cases of justice. In the earlier dialogues, this search is not usually successful. Plato makes more headway in the later dialogues, and the theory that such essences or Forms have an independent and objective existence gradually develops.

According to this theory, abstract general terms such as 'beauty', 'justice' and 'goodness' designate distinct, objective and independently existing entities or Forms. There is only a single Form for each such term. The Form is said to be 'present' in the many instances to which it correctly applies. Alternatively, they are said to 'share' or 'participate' in the Form. This is what makes them instances of it. Apart from metaphorical terms such as these, however, Plato does not succeed in elucidating the relation of the Forms to their instances.

Plato himself remains unclear about how widely this theory applies, as he implicity acknowledges in the *Parmenides* (132b–e).

---

[8] To illustrate this, Cornford cites the story of the French mathematician Pascal (*Before and after Socrates*, pp. 72–3). When he showed an intense interest in mathematics as a child, his father grew fearful that this would interfere with his other studies and forbade him any further access to the subject. Privately, the child set about discovering geometry for himself. He had made up his own axioms and definitions and proved thirty-two of Euclid's theorems before he was discovered.

The problem is partly due to the fact that the Theory of Forms is required to fulfil a wide variety of tasks in Plato's philosophy. In any case, he is undecided about which general terms designate Forms and which, if any, do not.

At the extreme, Plato sometimes seems to suggest that there is a Form for every general term. In recapping the theory in Book X he says, 'we always postulate in each case a single form for each set of particular things, to which we apply the same name' (596a).[9] The interpretation of these lines is disputed; normally the range of Forms is more restricted. In any case, the view that there is a Form for every general term is untenable as an account of Plato's views, since we can create general terms for entirely arbitrary and inessential groupings of things at will (for example, I can invent a term to describe all heavy blue objects). For Plato, however, it is clear that the Theory of Forms is not an abstract logical theory about the meaning of general terms; it involves an essentialist metaphysical theory about the nature of reality.

Plato admits his uncertainty about the range of terms which designate Forms. Normally it appears to include at least beauty, justice and goodness (the central examples in the *Republic*), some very general notions such as Identity and Difference, Being and non-Being, the One and the Many, etc., and usually some notions of natural species and kinds, such as human being, ox and stone. Mathematical notions, such as numbers and geometric figures, are at times treated by Plato as Forms.[10] In Book X Plato also holds that there are Forms of human products such as tables and couches (I will discuss such cases presently).

The theory that general terms designate independent entities is usually called logical 'realism'. This is confusing, since what it deems 'real' are ideal entities: Forms or universals known only to thought. As a metaphysical doctrine the Theory of Forms is a species of essentialism. It asserts that there are common properties or essences which make things the sorts of things that they are. Different species and kinds exist objectively and our language and theory describe them more or less correctly. A true theory, as Plato

---

[9] See also *Letter* VII, 342d, and *Parmenides* 130c–d.
[10] There are problems about this which are beyond the scope of this book. See Cross and Woozley, *Plato's* Republic, pp. 233–8.

graphically puts it, cuts nature 'at the joints', whereas a false account 'mangles the parts' (*Phaedrus* 265d).

Such views have been widely challenged ever since Plato's time. Many philosophers in the empiricist and materialist traditions are sceptical of the existence of intelligible entities such as Forms or universals. According to Locke, for example, 'universality belongs not to things themselves which are all of them particular in their existence'. It is we who create universality, by grouping particulars together under a single common term. Universals, he says, are mere 'inventions and creatures of the understanding'.[11] Likewise, the essentialist idea that nature has objective 'joints' and that there are objective divisions and kinds is widely rejected. The division of the world into different species and kinds, it is argued, is conventional and arbitrary, the result only of our particular way of seeing things. There are no essences in the world.

These views raise issues for Plato's approach which are too large to deal with here. However, it would be wrong to leave the impression that essentialist views have no current influence. Many contemporary scientists hold Platonic views about their work. They reject the view that their theories are nothing but conventional 'ways of seeing things'. As Plato suggests, they are attempting to delineate the essential nature of things, to cut reality at its joints. Again Hegel puts the point well. In the sciences, he says, 'objective reality is attributed to laws, forces are immanent ... Genera, too ... are not just groupings of similarities, an abstraction made by us: they ... are the object's own inner essence ... Physics looks upon these universals as its triumph.'[12]

Forms as Ideals

Forms also function as ideal standards. According to Plato, knowledge of the Form of justice provides the Guardians with a 'pattern' or 'standard' (*paradeigma*) of perfection by which they guide society (484c). But the most extended use of the notion of Forms as ideals is in Book X, in the course of Plato's account of the nature

---

[11] Locke, *Essay concerning Human Understanding*, III.iii.11. Elsewhere, and inconsistently with this, Locke talks of 'real essences'.

[12] Hegel, *Philosophy of Nature*, p. 10.

of poetry. This starts with a general account of the products of human craftwork, such as beds and tables. Elsewhere Plato indicates that he has doubts about whether there are Forms for such objects, but any such doubts are absent here. There is a single Form of a bed which serves as an ideal standard. The carpenter works 'with his eye on the Form' (596b). The particular bed that results is said to 'copy', 'resemble' or 'approximate to' the Form more or less adequately. The Form functions as an ideal exemplar. The implication seems to be that the Form of Beauty, for example, is something perfectly beautiful, the Form of Justice is ideally just, and so on.

A celebrated logical paradox is evident here for the Theory of Forms. Plato was aware of the problem; it is discussed in the *Parmenides* (132a–b) and it has exercised philosophers ever since. Since Aristotle it has come to be known as the problem of the 'third man'. According to the Theory of Forms, particular men are men in virtue of participating in the Form of man. If the Form of man is itself a man, then we seem to need to posit a third Form of man in virtue of which the Form of man is itself a man, and so on *ad infinitum*.

In order to avoid this paradox the Form must not have itself as an instance. The Form of Man must not itself be a man, the Form of Beauty cannot be beautiful, and so forth. The Form must not be predicated of itself since this leads to paradox and absurdity. There has been a huge amount of controversy about how Plato's theory should be interpreted in the light of this and of the logical issues involved, but further discussion is beyond the scope of the present work.

The Form of the Good

In any case, the Forms function as ideals. Hence a knowledge of the Forms gives us an understanding not only of how the world is but also of how it ought to be. A full and true knowledge of reality in Plato's view ultimately has a moral dimension.

In this respect, Plato's account of knowledge conflicts with the modern scientific conception of it. For science, according to the modern view, tells us of facts but not of values. According to Plato, by contrast, the ultimate goal, the highest knowledge is of the essential nature of goodness: the Form of the Good. This is what the Guardians must ultimately strive towards if they are to have a proper understanding of justice and the social good.

However, when challenged to explain the Form of the Good, Plato admits that the task is beyond him (506d). He offers instead an account of what he calls 'a child of the good', something which 'resembles it very closely' (506e): the analogy of the sun (507a–509c). This is one of the most suggestive but at the same time obscure passages in the whole of the *Republic*. To appreciate it, one must first put aside the modern idea that goodness is subjective, a matter of mere preference. For Plato, it is an objective feature of things themselves.

Just as the sun is supreme in the sensible world, so the Form of the Good is supreme in the realm of thought. Just as the sun's light makes objects visible to the eye, so the Form of the Good makes objects intelligible and enables them to be known. And, just as the sun is the source not only of things' visibility, but also of their existence and growth, so the Form of the Good is the ultimate source of the existence and reality of things.

Plato's account here contrasts fundamentally with the naturalistic and materialistic outlook of contemporary science. As Cornford puts it,

> Platonism seeks the key to Nature, not in the beginning, but in the end – not in mechanical causes impelling from behind, but in final causes which attract (as it were from in front) a movement of desire towards a pattern of ideal perfection.[13]

In other words, what Plato seems to be suggesting with the image of the sun is an all-encompassing teleological vision of the world which is best understood in religious terms.[14] In this the Form of the Good plays a role like that of God as the ultimate creative source of order and values.

All things aim towards perfection. In so doing, they participate in an overall design or purpose, which is for the Good. As with Plato's account of society, an organic conception is involved here, but it is now worked out on a cosmic scale. Just as individuals, by fulfilling their social role (which is their good), contribute to the

---

[13] Cornford, *Before and after Socrates*, pp. 63–4.
[14] A teleological view is one which portrays things as aimed towards an end.

good of society, so all things have an essential role in the whole scheme of things and, by fulfilling it, contribute to the ultimate purpose. All the lesser Forms – including justice and beauty – are part of this scheme; all contribute to the supreme end, which is realisation of the Good. To have full knowledge of a thing is to see it as part of this scheme and to understand it as adapted to the fulfilment of this end. Knowledge of the nature of things is thus at the same time knowledge of their purpose, end or value. Science and morality, fact and value, are, for Plato, inseparable.

In response to the charge that this approach involves deriving values from facts, an 'ought' from an 'is', and that it thus commits the 'naturalistic fallacy', Plato would no doubt have pleaded guilty. The teleological vision suggested by the analogy of the sun does, indeed, involve a form of ethical naturalism. But it is not thereby fallacious. Naturalism – the view that values are grounded in facts about the nature of things – is a perfectly coherent and defensible philosophical stance. According to Plato's cosmic version of it, an evaluative end – the Good – is inscribed in the very fabric of things themselves as its highest organising principle and most fundamental law. And grasping this rational order by gaining a knowledge of the Form of the Good is the highest aim of knowledge.

Some Practical Implications

These ideas have had a profound and enduring impact on the whole history of European philosophy from Aristotle onwards. They have been particularly influential on religious thought. It is often said that in the modern era the teleological picture has been refuted and replaced by the scientific approach. This involves what Weber graphically describes as a 'disenchanted' view of the world. It sees natural events as the result of material causes without any larger organisation, end or purpose. But even in the face of modern science, the Platonic approach still has defenders. Like Kant, they maintain that there are questions about moral values and the ultimate order of things which cannot be answered by science. It is necessary to limit the claims of modern science to be the sole form of knowledge. Properly understood, the scientific and the teleological accounts do not conflict and there is room for both.

When Plato gives his account of justice as harmony in society and the self in Book V, he describes it as a 'mere sketch' lacking 'precision' and warns that we must make a detour and travel a longer route to attain more exact knowledge (435c–d, 504a–e). We have now travelled that route; but what have we learned about the nature of justice as a result? The Theory of Forms is undoubtedly fertile and important in metaphysics, epistemology and even in religious thought, but what does it contribute to the understanding of morals and politics?

The view that everything has its place in the larger scheme of things is sometimes said to be inherently conservative. That is not necessarily so. In an imperfect world, change is just as much a part of the rational order of things and for the good as preservation of the *status quo*, particularly where the existing situation is harmful or rotten.

More validly, it is argued that the Theory of Forms in the end adds little to Plato's earlier account of morality and politics. Partly, this is due to problems of Plato's apparent dualism, which I have already discussed. If the intelligible realm of the Forms is treated as 'another world', independent of the world of the senses, then it is difficult to see how a knowledge of Forms can be of any practical relevance to the this-worldly problems of moral and social life.

But there are deeper problems as well. Despite the central place of the Theory of Forms in the argument of the *Republic*, all that it appears to yield in the end is the vague and elusive image of the sun, which adds little specific to the earlier account of justice as harmony. There are surely good grounds for Popper's charge that 'Plato's Idea of the Good is practically empty. It gives us no indication of what is good.'[15]

The reason for this may be as follows. Plato seems to be telling us to see all things as part of a larger rational order. If this means that whatever exists or happens must be regarded as rational and right, then it is impossible to criticise any situation, no matter how evil it may appear to be; and this philosophy has no specific practical implications whatsoever.[16]

---

[15]   *The Open Society*, Vol. I, p. 274 n. 32.

[16]   Similar problems afflict the Hegelian doctrine that what is actual is rational, see Sayers, *Marxism and Human Nature*, Ch. 6, for further discussion.

Guide to Further Reading

Other dialogues in which Plato develops the Theory of Forms include the *Phaedo* and the *Meno*. There is an obscure but important critical discussion in the *Parmenides*. Grube, *Plato's Thought*, Chapter 1, gives a good brief overview of Plato's Theory of Forms covering the whole span of his work.

Cornford, *Before and after Socrates*, Chapter 3, contains a classic brief and popular account of Plato's approach, setting it usefully in the context of the development of Greek philosophy. Excellent general accounts of the Theory of Forms are given in A. Wedberg, 'The Theory of Ideas', and H. F. Cherniss, 'The Philosophical Economy of the Theory of Ideas'. Nettleship, *Lectures*, Chapter 10, gives an eloquent account of the teleological vision of the Theory of Forms, particularly as it is embodied in the analogy of the sun.

Accounts focused more on the logical aspects of Plato's theory can be found in Annas, *Introduction to Plato's* Republic, Chapters 8–9, Vlastos, 'Degrees of Reality in Plato', and Cross and Woozley, *Plato's* Republic, Chapters 7–8.

11 The Line, the Cave and Higher Education (VI.509d–VII.541b)

According to Plato the supreme aim of philosophy is to comprehend the Form of the Good. His attention now turns to the process of education by which the select group of Guardians can be led up to this knowledge.

In the light of the distinctions introduced by the Theory of Forms, it is clear that the first stage of education in music and the arts described in Book III (see Chapter 4 above) never reaches beyond the world of the senses. Its aim is to ensure that its recipients hold correct beliefs about this world and about the gods. The higher education which is now to be described is designed to detach the mind from the world of the senses and to introduce it to the intelligible world of the Forms. Its ultimate purpose is to lead the mind up to a knowledge of the Form of the Good. Plato describes this progress with two celebrated images: the divided line and the cave.

The Divided Line (509d–511e)

Plato asks us to picture a line divided into two unequal parts (A+B, C+D), each of which is then subdivided again in the same proportions. The resulting four sections (A, B, C, D) correspond to four states of mind or modes of cognition, each clearer and more certain than the one below. These are stages through which the mind must pass as it acquires knowledge. Corresponding to these are four kinds of 'objects' (see Figure 11.1) – although here, as before (p. 112), it is unclear whether we are to think of these as

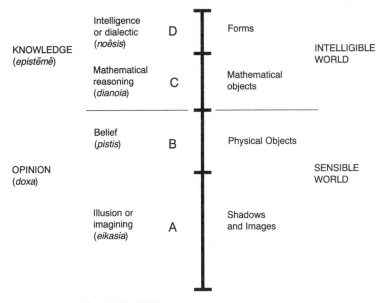

Figure 11.1 The Divided Line

distinct and different entities or rather as different aspects or views which the world presents.

A. The first and lowest level of cognition, corresponding to the first segment of the line, is termed *eikasia* by Plato. There is no clear equivalent for this in English. According to Cornford, 'it is etymologically connected with *eikon* = image, likeness, and with *eikos* = likely, and it can mean either likeness (representation) or likening (comparison) or estimation of likelihood (conjecture)'.[1] It is rendered in modern translations by terms such as 'illusion' (Lee) or 'imagining' (Cornford).

In any case, this is the word used by Plato to describe our initial and least enlightened state of mind, in which we take appearances and common representations and opinions for reality. We all begin by perceiving the appearances which things present, and construing the world in terms of images and representations. It is also the initial condition of the prisoners in the cave while they are still chained in their places and see only shadows.

---

[1] *Republic*, trans. Cornford, p. 222.

The earliest stage of education is adapted to this state of mind: it works with stories and images. Different people will advance to different levels of knowledge beyond it in different areas of thought during the course of their lives. Only a few, Plato believes, achieve the highest level.

B. The next stage of cognition is 'belief' (*pistis*). This involves awareness of objects and not just of their images and representations. Nevertheless, it remains a type of 'opinion' (*doxa*) based on acquaintance with sensible particulars; it is not yet 'knowledge' of Forms. The views about justice put forward by Cephalus and Polemarchus in Book I are examples of 'belief'. They define justice by citing particular examples and principles of just actions, but do not grasp the Form, the nature of justice itself. It is the state of mind which the first stage of education tries to create by inculcating correct beliefs about what is virtuous and about the behaviour of the gods. This is the condition of the young Guardians before their higher education. Plato calls it 'true opinion without understanding' and says that a person in this state is like 'a blind man on the right road' (506c).

C. Through a training in mathematics and then in philosophy, higher education is designed to free the mind from the realm of sensible appearances and introduce it to the intelligible world of the Forms. The first stage of this process is exemplified by mathematical reasoning (*dianoia*). Two characteristics of this are mentioned.

First, mathematics does not deal with Forms directly, but employs sensible images and representations of them. Plato cites the use of diagrams in what we now call Euclidean geometry, though he suggests that such images are an essential part of all mathematical reasoning.[2] In a geometric proof reference must be made to a diagram – for example, to a triangle ABC – but the proof concerns triangles in general and not only the particular figure in the diagram. The diagram is a mere image which is supposed to represent the triangle as such, the intelligible Form of the triangle, which is the true subject of geometric reasoning. Geometry (and other kinds of mathematical reasoning in so far as they resemble it)

---

[2] Euclid lived about half a century after Plato. It was only in the seventeenth century that Descartes first showed that geometric figures can be described by a system of coordinates and results about them derived in abstract algebraic terms without reference to a diagram.

thus forms a bridge by which the mind can pass from the world of the senses to the intelligible realm of the Forms.

Second, mathematical reasoning (*dianoia*) is a form of thought which depends upon 'hypotheses' or 'assumptions' (Lee), suppositions which are simply taken as given without proof. Exactly what Plato means by this is not clear, and I shall come back to this question later in the chapter. In any case, he does not mean that such reasoning is doubtful or provisional. On the contrary, he believed that the geometry and mathematics of his time were true of their objects (space and number).

D. These two limitations are overcome in the fourth and final stage of cognition, which Plato calls dialectic. This is a purely rational sort of knowledge involving no input from the senses. At this level, the aid of visible diagrams or illustrations is left behind and the mind deals only with the intelligible Forms themselves. Moreover, knowledge at this level no longer relies on hypotheses. It has attained a 'synoptic' vision which grasps all the elements of reality as a whole, unified ultimately under one supreme unconditioned principle, presumably the Form of the Good. (I will return to this topic below).

The Cave (514a–521b)

The Divided Line gives a structural and as it were 'static' account of the different stages of knowledge. The picture is given movement and life in the allegory of the cave. This describes the progress of the mind from ignorance to knowledge. Plato returns to the imagery of the sun and its light. He conceives of knowledge as a sort of illumination. He portrays the process of education as an ascent from darkness into light – as a passage from the perception of shadows and reflections towards the direct vision of objects and eventually of the source of light itself.

Plato portrays the initial and unenlightened condition of human consciousness as like that of prisoners confined since childhood in a dark cave. The prisoners are bound so that their gaze is fixed on the wall in front of them. Behind them, out of their view, is a fire in front of which some people manipulate puppets and other figures. All that the prisoners can see are the shadows these cast on the wall in front of them. In such circumstances the prisoners naturally take the flickering shadows they see for reality. When Glaucon protests that this is an 'odd picture', Plato replies that the prisoners are 'like us' (515a).

Some prisoners are now released – how or by whom is unclear. They are made to turn round and look at the fire. At first they find its light painful, dazzling and blinding. They resist and turn back towards the shadows. Similarly, if a prisoner is now dragged out of the cave and into the sunlight,

> the process would be a painful one, to which he would much object, and when he emerged into the light his eyes would be so dazzled by the glare of it that he would not be able to see a single one of the things he was now told were real.[3]

But once his eyes grow used to the sunlight, and his limbs to their new freedom, then he will begin to perceive things in the outside world, first by looking only at their shadows and reflections, but then by looking directly at the objects themselves. Eventually he may develop the ability to look at the source of light and the cause of things, the sun itself. And so he will come to appreciate his new condition and 'when he thought of his first home and what passed for wisdom there, and of his fellow-prisoners ... he would congratulate himself on his good fortune and be sorry for them' (516c).

This story, Plato tells us, should be interpreted in the light of the images of the sun and the Divided Line that precede it (517b). It is clear from this that it is an allegory of the process of enlightenment. The stages of the prisoners' journey out of the cave correspond to the divisions of the Line (see Figure 11.2).

The escape from the cave into the sunlight is one of the most powerful images in the whole of philosophical literature. It gives an inspiring and beautiful picture of the liberating and illuminating power of knowledge and education. Yet, as the story also suggests, education – particularly in demanding and difficult subjects such as philosophy – is seldom an effortless or immediately pleasurable experience. At first, at least, new knowledge is often confusing and unsettling. 'Compulsion' is needed, says Plato: those who are capable of acquiring it 'must be made to climb the ascent to the ... highest object of knowledge' (519c, Cornford translation).

---

[3] *Republic* 516a.

Divided Line	Cave
A. Illusion (*eikasia*)	Prisoners bound in the cave looking at shadows of puppets
B. Belief (*pistis*)	Prisoners freed in the cave seeing the puppets and the fire
C. Mathematical reason (*dianoia*)	Seeing shadows and reflections of objects outside the cave
D. Intelligence (*noēsis*)	Looking directly at objects outside the cave
Knowledge of the Form of the Good	Looking directly at the sun

Figure 11.2 The Line and the Cave

At the same time, Plato's allegory presents a bleak and pessimistic picture of the situation of the majority. For Plato explicitly maintains that most people are like the bound prisoners in the cave who see only a series of flickering shadows of puppets which they take for reality. Most of us, for most of our lives, live in ignorance and illusion (*eikasia*) from which we do not even want to escape.

Lee wonders whether Plato intends these claims to be taken seriously. Others object that there is no significant form of consciousness corresponding to the condition of *eikasia*.[4] But there is no reason to think that Plato does not mean what he says. Plato completely rejects what might be termed the 'Emperor's New Clothes' theory of knowledge, the simple empiricist view that reality is directly given to us in immediate experience. From birth

[4] *Republic*, trans. Lee, p. 317n. There is a useful discussion of this issue in Cross and Woozley, *Plato's* Republic, pp. 209–28.

our ordinary everyday consciousness is dominated by images, representations and fantasies largely drawn from popular culture and, nowadays, the media. These give a distorted and superficial view of things, a comforting veil of illusions which prevents us from grasping things as they really are.

The Return to the Cave

The allegory is not yet complete. Those who have struggled out of the cave and into the sunlight must now return. They are the chosen few who must put their knowledge to use to rule society. Again compulsion is needed. They do not wish to return. They would be happier to remain in the sunlight and devote themselves to purely intellectual pursuits. Moreover, those who do return will initially find it difficult to readapt to the darkness. They will seem blind and incompetent to the prisoners who have remained. The prisoners will scoff at their claims about the upper world and say that it has ruined their sight. And in a clear reference to the fate of Socrates, Plato adds, 'if anyone tried to release [the prisoners] and lead them up, they would kill him if they could lay hands on him' (517a).

Nevertheless, they must return. Plato has two reasons for insisting on this. In the first place, it is their social duty to return. The social good demands it. The mass of the people, Plato believes, lack the unifying direction which reason can give to life and are incapable of ruling themselves. On the other hand, those who spend their time contemplating purely intellectual matters are unwordly and equally unfit to rule. The philosophers must return and share the lives of the people if they are to be good rulers (519c–d).

When Glaucon protests that they will not be happy about this, he is reminded that the fundamental principle of the republic is to promote 'not the special welfare of any particular class ... but of the society as a whole' (519e, cf. 420d, 466a). In an unusually preachy passage which would not be out of place at a graduation ceremony today, Plato enunciates the moral implications.

> We have bred you both for your own sake and that of the whole community to act as leaders ... you are better and more fully educated than the rest and better qualified to combine the practice of philosophy and

politics. You must therefore each descend ... and live with your fellows in the cave and get used to seeing in the darkness ... and so our state ... will be really awake and not merely dreaming like most societies today.[5]

Plato is well aware of the Guardians' reluctance to return to the cave; but he regards this as a positive asset for them as rulers. The best rulers, he maintains, are those who are reluctant to rule and are not seeking a political career to gain power or riches (521a).

Plato's ambivalent feelings about the role of the philosopher are particularly evident in the present passage. Though the philosopher would prefer to remain out in the sunlight engaging in philosophy, the social interest demands a return to the cave and the duties of ruling. If the seventh *Letter* is to be believed, the conflict between a contemplative and a practical life was felt personally by Plato. He is often said to hold contradictory views on this topic. There is no doubt that he expresses differing views on the issue during the course of his work. In some dialogues (most notably the *Phaedo*) the scales are tipped strongly in favour of the contemplative conception of philosophy.

In the *Republic*, however, where the main topic is social philosophy, the practical view is unambiguously upheld. And not only for reasons of social duty. For Plato also implies that reason cannot be realised fully in mere intellectual contemplation, but only in practice, by actively bringing about good in the world. Its highest vocation is in ruling a society. This view is put forward most explicitly in the parable of the true navigator on the ship of drunken sailors. True philosophers, says Plato, suffer when they are excluded from using their abilities for the social good. They 'could do much more in a suitable society, where they could develop more fully, to their own salvation and that of the community' (497a).

As usual, Bloom has a quite different interpretation. He exaggerates Plato's ambivalence into a full-scale contradiction. The demands of philosophy and politics are irreconcilable, he maintains: to force the philosopher to return to the cave is 'unjust'. The very idea of a rational society governed by philosophy is an impossible ideal: 'the perfect society is a perfect impossibility'. Why then does Plato spend a whole book describing it? 'Precisely

---

[5] *Repubic* 520b–c.

to show its impossibility' according to Bloom. The work is intended ironically, it means the opposite of what it says. The striving for perfect justice 'puts unreasonable and despotic demands on ordinary men'. Human beings are flawed and imperfect.

> If the infinite longing for justice on earth is merely a dream or a prayer, the shedding of blood in its name turns from idealism into criminality. The revolutions of Communism or Fascism are made in the name of perfect regimes which are to be their consequence ... Socrates constructs his utopia to point up the dangers of what we would call utopianism; as such it is the greatest critique of political idealism ever written.[6]

As an account of Plato's philosophy this is absurd (unfortunately Bloom does not intend it ironically). Of course Plato believes in the validity of the ideal of a rationally ordered society. It is not a mere dream or prayer for him – he is a utopian social thinker. It is Bloom, not Plato, who rejects this ideal. No doubt Bloom is right to warn us of its dangers and to remind us of the imperfections of real human beings in the real world. Plato was not unaware of these matters as his account of 'imperfect' societies (in Books VIII–IX) shows; though perhaps he can be criticised for focusing too much on the ideal and paying too little attention to the problems of justice in the real world.[7]

What Plato is questioning, however, is whether people such as Bloom are right to believe that we must resign ourselves to this imperfect reality as the inevitable nature of things. Plato's main purpose is not to describe the actual world and its problems, but to present a guiding 'pattern', to give a vision of an ideal. Anyone who has glimpsed that vision will not be content with Bloom's dark view that selfish material concerns and social conflicts are inevitable, and that all we can hope for is a more or less satisfactory compromise between competing interests. They will strive towards Plato's vision of the sunlight outside the cave.

Dialectic

These central philosophical books of the dialogue conclude with a brief outline of the programme of higher education of the Guar-

---

[6] Bloom, 'Interpretive Essay', pp. 409–10.
[7] In the *Laws* Plato describes what he regards as a practically attainable ideal.

dians. As already noted, this starts with a training in mathematics and related subjects: arithmetic, plane and solid geometry, astronomy and harmonics (musical theory). The aim is not primarily practical, but rather to lead the mind up from the world of the senses to the intelligible world of the Forms. After ten years of this, from age 20 to 30, those selected to be Guardians are ready for philosophy and the final stage of knowledge, dialectic.

Plato's use of this term should not be confused with modern – Hegelian or Marxist – versions, though the latter draw substantially on the Platonic model. In Plato it has a less technical meaning which is closely related to its everyday sense of 'discourse' or 'discussion'. Plato's reference is to the process of question and answer by which he develops his philosophy. This involves questioning and criticising received opinions. For this reason Plato thinks that philosophy is dangerous for the young and he warns at length against introducing it too early (537d–539d). This is Plato's conservatism at work. The truth is that young people by themselves inevitably and naturally start to question established ideas when they reach a certain age, and philosophy can be particularly beneficial at this time.

In Plato, dialectic is both the highest stage of knowledge and the method by which it is achieved. It is the final stage of the journey out of the cave, the ultimate aim of which is to look directly at the sun itself, to attain a vision of the Form of the Good. Plato attempts to describe this in two brief passages (510c–511d, 533a–534e); but he admits that he cannot give a satisfactory or full account (533a). Unfortunately, these passages are too sketchy and obscure to resolve many of the controversies which they have provoked.

Plato explains dialectic by contrast with mathematical reasoning. It is a purely rational sort of knowledge which does not require the use of visible diagrams. In it the mind deals only with the intelligible Forms themselves. And it does not rely upon hypotheses.

I will take the latter point first. As was mentioned above, there has been a great deal of controversy about what Plato means by it. It is clear that he is not using the term 'hypothesis' in its modern sense, which would imply that the basis of mathematical reasoning is provisional or doubtful. On the contrary, he believed that the geometry and mathematics of his time were true of their objects, space and number.[8]

Sometimes he is taken to be referring to the axiomatic structure of mathematics. This was first demonstrated about half a century after Plato's death by Euclid. He showed that geometry can be presented as a formal system of theorems which can be deduced logically from a small number of apparently self-evident assumptions or axioms. On this interpretation, the non-hypothetical aspirations of Plato's dialectic would involve a search for certainty, that is, for proof of these axioms and hence for the 'foundations' of mathematics.

The search for such foundations has been a major preoccupation of modern philosophy but there are no indications that this is Plato's project. Moreover, it is doubtful that his concerns are of this formal and logical character. Plato's notion of dialectic is better understood in the light of the metaphysics of the Theory of Forms. As we have seen, this involves the view that reality is a single whole which forms an organic sort of unity.

Philosophy, for Plato, is distinguished by its 'comprehensive' or 'synoptic' approach (537c, cf. 531d). It comprehends things fully and as they truly are. In the light of Plato's metaphysics, it must be seen as involving an understanding of things as elements in the whole and as necessarily related to other things in the context of the whole. Mathematical reasoning falls short of this synoptic vision. Geometry, for example, considers only the spatial aspect of things, abstracted from all other characteristics. Moreover, it takes its starting point, spatiality, as a mere datum, as an unexplained and independently given element without any essential connection with other things.

Dialectic, says Plato, 'destroys' hypotheses (533c). There has been much debate about the meaning of this enigmatic phrase. It could mean that dialectic 'refutes' the hypotheses on which mathematical reasoning is based; but that seems unlikely since Plato is not challenging the validity of mathematics or geometry. More plausibly, Plato can be taken to mean that dialectic destroys these hypotheses *as* hypotheses. Mathematics is hypothetical in the sense that it takes its objects as ultimate, although in reality they are part of a larger whole and dependent on external conditions. By

---

[8] It is now thought that space is more accurately described in non-Euclidean terms.

exposing these conditions, dialectic reveals their hypothetical character and leads to a search for the higher conditions on which they depend.

The rational mind, Plato believes, constantly seeks for the conditions or principles of things, for their connection with other things in the wider unity of the whole. It is thus led on from condition to condition, from principle to principle. Through dialectic the mind ascends through a series of such principles. Ultimately it reaches a supreme principle which is 'not hypothetical' (511b), not in the sense that it is absolutely certain, but rather in the sense that it is not conditional on anything external to it. This is the unconditioned, the first principle of all things, which Plato calls the Form of the Good.

This then provides the starting point for the 'downward' path which comprises the second part of Plato's dialectical method. From this non-hypothetical first principle, Plato maintains, it is now possible to deduce all the specific branches and particular elements of knowledge (511b). Full knowledge thus involves seeing all things as products of the Good, in their relation to the whole and not dependent upon anything outside it.

The other point of contrast between dialectic and mathematical reasoning is also illuminated by this interpretation. Dialectic, Plato says, 'involves nothing in the sensible world, but moves solely through forms to forms, and finishes with forms' (511b–c). Unlike mathematics, it makes no appeal to visible images or representations: it is purely rational and a priori. If the above account is correct, Plato does not mean that philosophical knowledge is, to use the modern term, 'analytic'. He is not asserting that philosophical claims lack any empirical content and depend only upon meanings for their truth. Quite the contrary. When we comprehend the Form of the Good we understand the supreme principle, the reason, the necessity of *all* things. As Nettleship explains,

> In perfect knowledge there would be no element of sense; not that anything which our senses tell us would be lost sight of, but that every sensible property of the object would be seen as the manifestation of some

intelligible form; so that there would be no . . . irrelevant element in it, and it would have become perfectly intelligible.[9]

Guide to Further Reading

Nettleship, *Lectures*, Chapters 11–12, contains an eloquent and influential discussion of these sections to which I am particularly indebted. H. W. B. Joseph criticises this account in *Knowledge and the Good in Plato's* Republic, Chapters 4–5. Other helpful accounts of the Divided Line and the cave can be found in: Annas, *Introduction to Plato's* Republic, Chapters 10–11; Cross and Woozley, *Plato's* Republic, Chapters 9–10; and Crombie, *Examination of Plato's Doctrines*, Volume I, Chapter 3 Section 5 (see also Volume II, pp. 171–97).

Bloom's account of the return to the cave is to be found in his 'Interpretative Essay', pp. 407–12. This is well criticised by Hall, 'The *Republic* and the "Limits of Politics"'.

Plato's dialectical method and the role of 'hypothesis' in his account of knowledge is usefully discussed by R. Robinson, 'Hypothesis in the *Republic*'. An account of the sort he gives, which I have broadly adopted, is criticised by R. G. Collingwood, *An Essay on Philosophical Method*, pp. 10–17.

---

[9] *Lectures*, pp. 255–6.

12 The Reply to the Sophists (VIII.543a–IX.592b)

The long 'digression' of Books V–VII is at an end. At the beginning of Book VIII the argument is resumed precisely from where it was interrupted at the start of Book V (449a). Books VIII–IX effectively constitute the conclusion to the main argument of the dialogue. They are Plato's final response to the initial challenge of Glaucon and Adeimantus. Important though it is, the remainder of the dialogue (Book X) is a sort of appendix.

Plato's earlier account has shown that justice is a sort of mental health, and hence good in itself. To round off his argument, Plato now plans to contrast justice in society and the individual with various different kinds of injustice in order to show that justice is preferable.

The Decline of Society and the Self (543a–576b)

As Plato observes, there is only a single kind of just society – the ideal republic described earlier – whereas injustice takes many forms (445c). Conveniently, Plato narrows these down to four basic kinds: timarchy, oligarchy, democracy and tyranny. He gives a vivid account of these as if they follow on from the ideal society in a historical sequence of corruption and decline. As with the account of the formation of society in Book II, however, it is unclear how far this is intended as an account of actual historical developments.[1] Although there is a good deal of realistic detail

---

[1] This is how Aristotle appears to take this passage which he criticises for its historical inaccuracies, *Politics* 1315b–1316b.

Society	Ruling part of the self		
Ideal	Reason		
Timarchy	Spirit		
Oligarchy		necessary	
Democracy	Appetites	unnecessary	
Tyranny		lawless	

Figure 12.1 Types of Society and Forms of the Self

drawn from Greek politics, Plato's primary purpose is analytical and philosophical. These different types of society form a *moral* order, from the best (Plato's ideal republic) to the worst (tyranny). They exhibit an increasing degree of disunity as reason loses control and the appetites achieve freer and freer reign.

In contrast to the idea of progress which dominates modern historical thought, Plato sees history as a process of decline from an original Golden Age. Moreover, he distinguishes different types of society by their ruling classes rather than by the form of their political constitutions. In this respect, it might be thought, his political philosophy has an affinity with Marxism. For Plato, however, the nature of the ruling class is not a socio-economic but a psychological matter. Types of society are distinguished by the part of the self which is predominant in the personality of its rulers (see Figure 12.1).

Plato follows his usual method of first describing the society and only then the associated individual type. By starting with the 'larger' phenomenon, as Plato puts it, we get a clearer form of presentation; but this procedure also embodies the idea that individual character is a product of society rather than vice versa, as the individualist claims.[2]

The sequence that Plato now describes starts with his ideal republic. This has the constitutional form of an Aristocracy (literally, rule by the best) or, if there is only one ruler, a Monarchy (445d), although the rulers are selected by merit and not by birth.

[2] See pp. 20–1 above.

The associated character type is that of the philosopher-ruler.

Starting from the ideal immediately presents Plato with a problem. As ideal it should be immune from change; its corruption is thus inexplicable. Since philosophy fails him here, he seeks inspiration from the 'Muses'. As when he has recourse to myth this is Plato's way of expressing ideas which he believes to be true, but for which he lacks proof. In any case, the story as he tells it presumes that nothing actual is fully ideal: 'all created things must decay' (546a). Divisions somehow arise among the Guardians and deterioration sets in. Eventually private property is instituted for them and social antagonism between rulers and ruled develops. The process of decline has begun.

Timarchy is the first result. Plato invents this term to describe a society in which the values of spirit – courage and honour (*timē*) – replace those of reason. Specifically, he has in mind the militaristic type of society which existed at the time in Sparta and Crete (544c). Such societies are associated with a 'timarchic' personality in which spirit is the dominant part of the self. This kind of person is energetic and ambitious but lacks confidence in their own authority.

Timarchy is replaced in its turn by Oligarchy. Literally, this means 'rule by a few', but the word is used here to mean rule by a wealthy elite. Wealth is now the basis of power and privilege, and the principle that rulers are selected for their abilities is abandoned. The society becomes split into two hostile groups of rich and poor, and weakened as a result.

The oligarchic personality is dominated by the 'necessary' appetites. Such a person subordinates everything, including their own comforts, to the accumulation of wealth. This is reminiscent of the character type of the early capitalist as described by Weber, who is imbued with the ascetic values of the Protestant work ethic.[3] Plato's account raises the important question of what are 'necessary' appetites. I shall return to this later in this chapter.

Oligarchic society also sees the first emergence of people who perform no useful social function and are mere consumers. Such people may be either wealthy or poor, either rich idlers or paupers, beggars and criminals. In either case Plato regards them as mere

[3] M. Weber, *The Protestant Ethic and the Spirit of Capitalism.*

'drones', at best useless but often positively harmful to society (552a–c). Plato's theory that people are essentially social beings is evident here. He holds a 'producer' rather than a 'consumer' ethic, according to which we can realise ourselves fully only by contributing usefully to the community.

The next stage of decline is what Plato calls 'democracy' (literally, rule by the people). His picture is such an unsympathetic caricature that it is unclear whether he has democratic Athens in mind. He describes a state of anarchic licence in which social order and authority have broken down completely and people can do as they please. Likewise, the democratic personality is anarchic and disordered. It is dominated by the 'unnecessary' desires, by an undisciplined and promiscuous pursuit of any and every passing appetite and whim.

This anarchy finally results in the coming to power of an absolute despot or tyrant. Plato paints a powerful and compelling picture of the tyrannical personality. This is a personality in which all restraint is abandoned and in which 'lawless' – incestuous and murderous – desires now surface. In the normal personality these are suppressed and appear only in dreams; but in the tyrant they emerge and gain expression. Similarities with Freud's picture of the hidden depths of the self are striking. The tyrant becomes isolated, fearful and, eventually, enslaved by a single lustful 'master passion'.

The Comparison of Justice with Injustice (576b–592b)

The stage is now set for Plato to weigh the claims of justice and injustice against each other. His aim is to vindicate his initial assertion that justice rather than injustice is desirable not only for its consequences but also in itself, and thus answer the challenge made to him at the beginning by Glaucon and Adeimantus. He gives three arguments to this effect.

The first follows directly from the account he has just given of the different sorts of society and their associated personality types. Plato invites us to compare the happiness of the perfectly just person – the philosophical Guardian in his ideal society – with the completely unjust person, the tyrant. Initially, it may well seem, the tyrant is the happier. He (or it may be she) is all powerful. They can do whatever they want and have whatever they want. They should be free and wealthy. In reality, Plato argues, they are neither happy, nor free, nor wealthy.

In the first place, they are not free, they are a slave to their passions: their self is 'enslaved and completely controlled by a minority of the lowest and most lunatic impulses' (577d). Nor is the democratic personality much better off: it is dragged here and there by every whim and fancy.

Freedom is not a major value for Plato. However, what he says about it here is noteworthy in that it anticipates the 'positive conception' of liberty developed by subsequent philosophers.[4] Freedom for Plato is connected with the idea of the harmony of the self. It does not consist in the mere absence of restraint – the liberty to satisfy any and every desire. That is the false, merely negative, freedom of the democratic personality. Rather, as Nettleship puts it, freedom resides in the positive power 'to satisfy those desires in which the whole self finds satisfaction'.[5]

Furthermore the tyrant is not truly wealthy. It is a mistake to think that wealth consists simply in the accumulation of material goods. Plato implies instead that wealth is relative to our appetites and their satisfaction. Though tyrants have abundant material riches at their disposal, their appetites and desires are endless. They are never satisfied and always in want, always in need. People with fewer and simpler material needs, by contrast, are more easily satisfied; they can develop other aspects of the self and are the truly wealthy ones. The tyrant, moreover, is not content but lives in constant fear and insecurity.

In short, contrary to what Thrasymachus maintains at the beginning of the dialogue, injustice is not the way to happiness. The most unjust sort of person – the tyrant – is the least happy, while the just life is the happiest. And contrary to what Glaucon initially claims, a person's reputation makes no difference to this. Thus Plato answers the Sophists.

The first argument appeals to Glaucon's judgement about which sort of life is more worthwhile; but others might judge differently.

---

[4] See, e.g., T. H. Green, 'Lecture on Liberal Legislation and Freedom of Contract'.
[5] *Lectures*, p. 137.

The next two arguments are designed to show that the just life – the life of the philosopher (Plato shifts focus here) – is objectively preferable. The problem is that different kinds of person find different kinds of pleasure in different styles of life depending on which part of the self is dominant in them. There are philosophical types in whom reason predominates, ambitious and competitive characters dominated by spirit, and appetitive people whose main enjoyments come from material wealth and consumption. Each gets pleasure from their own way of life and prefers it to the others. How can we assess which really involves the greater pleasure?

The judgement, says Plato, must be made on the basis of 'experience, intelligence and reason' (582a). Of the three types of person, only the philosophers have experience of all three sorts of pleasure, since only they know the pleasures of rational thought. Furthermore, only they are fully able to bring intelligence and reason to bear on their experience. The philosophers are thus best qualified to judge and, not surprisingly, they judge their own style of life – the life of reason – to be the one that is truly preferable.

Mill employs a similar argument to show that 'higher' pleasures are preferable to 'lower' ones and that it is 'better to be Socrates dissatisfied than a fool satisfied'.[6] The argument is highly controversial in both cases. Pleasure is a purely subjective feeling, it is said; it makes no sense to try to compare different people's pleasures in this fashion. If a person prefers some way of life other than that of Socrates and claims to get greater pleasure from it, then no one can validly say they are mistaken. So it is often argued. But Plato disputes this, and so does Mill. Their point is that only a person who has experience of the alternatives and has thought intelligently about them is in a position to make an informed and valid judgement.

Also questionable, it may be thought, is the view that the philosopher has the widest experience. One must recall that Plato, at least, is thinking not of a modern academic who, for the most part, leads a narrow and cloistered life but of the philosopher-ruler in his ideal society. But still the claim is dubious and it is difficult to dispel the suspicion that this argument is merely the self-justification of the philosopher.

[6] Mill, *Utilitarianism*, p. 260.

The third argument raises equally controversial issues. Plato distinguishes true from false, real from illusory, pleasures in order to demonstrate that the philosophical life leads to the truest and most genuine sort of satisfaction. The pleasures which come from gratification of the appetites are illusory (583b–587b). They are always mixed with pain. They arise only through contrast with the pain of want which they relieve. The pleasure of eating, for example, comes by contrast with the pain of hunger and is always connected with it. Most (but not all) bodily pleasures are of this sort. Intellectual pleasures, in contrast, are 'true' pleasures. They are pure pleasures which are desired for themselves and not solely as a relief from pain.

A further argument is based on the metaphysics of the Theory of Forms. As we have seen, this theory holds that physical objects – the objects of the appetites and the senses – are not fully real: they are changeable and transient. The pleasures which come from physical things – the pleasures of appetite – are similarly unreal: they are fleeting and passing. The satisfaction of a desire like hunger, for example, is only temporary; soon the desire reappears, the hunger returns and the self is unchanged.

The only full reality is the eternal and unchanging realm of the Forms which we can know only through the use of reason. The pleasures which come from rational knowledge of the Forms, argues Plato, are also real: they are permanent and lasting. Thus understanding and knowledge develop in the individual in a cumulative and progressive manner so that the self is permanently changed and enhanced by them.

The Concept of False Pleasure

A number of problems are raised by these arguments. It is questionable whether the pleasures of reason really are more lasting than those of appetite. Are hunger and the appetite for knowledge really so different in this respect? Arguably, satisfaction of the desire for knowledge creates the desire for more knowledge, thus, as with hunger, merely reproducing the desire. If so, the hope that Plato holds out, of a state of permanent satisfaction in which our desires are stilled, is illusory.

This view is forcefully expressed by Callicles in the *Gorgias*, which contains an excellent discussion of these arguments. On the Platonic view that happiness consists in the absence of desire, Callicles says, 'stones and corpses would be supremely happy' (492).[7] Desire is the very essence of life, and the best life consists of having large and varied appetites and enjoying their satisfaction (494).[8]

Moreover, even if we accept that physical objects are changeable and therefore in some sense 'unreal', and that the pleasures derived from them are transitory, it does not follow that these pleasures are unreal. Indeed, the very idea of an unreal or illusory pleasure is problematic. In one sense, everything felt is 'real'. Plato is clearly not denying the reality of the pleasures of appetite in that sense; he is not suggesting that such pleasures are not felt. Rather, he means that they are unreal in the sense that they are based on illusion. Drug-induced pleasure (like that in Brave New World, for example) or pleasure felt in a dream, give some idea of Plato's meaning.[9]

Difficult issues are involved here. On the one hand, one may question whether such pleasures are illusory. They are, after all, felt, and 'real' in that sense – the self *is* pleased. Can a dream not cause real fright and terror? If so, why not real pleasure? On the other hand, Plato does seem to have a point when he insists that there is something particularly insubstantial and illusory about the pleasures of dreams, and that satisfaction based on true understanding is in some sense more genuine.

Attitudes to Wealth

Whatever one makes of these arguments, Plato's hostility to the appetites is clear. He appears to denigrate them and deny that their satisfaction contributes anything to happiness. At times he seems almost to want to suppress them or, at least, to escape from them altogether.[10]

However, this conflicts with other strands of his thought. It

[7] Hobbes, likewise, rejects the idea of a '*summum bonum*' as he calls the Platonic ideal. 'The felicity of this life consists not in the repose of a mind satisfied ... Nor can a man any more live whose desires are at an end than he whose senses and imagination are at a stand ... so that I put for a general inclination of all mankind a perpetual and restless desire of power after power that ceases only in death. (*Leviathan*, pp. 122–3)

[8] Nietzsche echoes this when he denounces Plato's philosophy as opposed to 'life', *Twilight of the Idols*, p. 39; see also *The Birth of Tragedy*, Sections 12–15.

[9] For Plato, however, even the fully conscious pleasures of appetite are illusory. Pleasures from drug experience or dreams are doubly illusory: illusions based on illusions.

[10] This is what Callicles and Nietzsche are criticising. This theme is particularly marked in the *Phaedo* where Socrates is portrayed as looking forward to death as a release from the body and its limitations.

cannot be reconciled with the view that some appetites are 'necessary'; and it does not sit happily with Plato's ideal of the harmonious self. For the idea of harmony implies that at least the necessary appetites play an essential part in happiness and must be given their due.

Even if we do not take Plato to be entirely dismissing the contribution of the appetites to happiness, it is evident that he sees their proper place in the self as lowly and subordinate. Just as the productive class is the 'lower' and 'worse' part of society, so are the appetites in the self. Any growth of them beyond the unavoidable minimum is dangerous and evil, a threat, to psychological harmony and happiness.

Plato's attitude to wealth can be seen as a response to changes which were occurring in Greek society; but it can also be located in a wider context. The idea that there are inherent and natural limits to the desirable development of wealth is typically premodern. Throughout the ancient and medieval periods the word 'luxury' (with the sense of the excessive indulgence of appetites) denotes a vice. Attempts were constantly being made to limit commerce, trade and the growth of wealth.

The modern world, by contrast, is dominated by the view that the appetites of the individual and the wealth of nations can and should grow indefinitely. Since the Enlightenment, the mainstream of modern thought has embraced the idea of material progress. Luxury is no longer looked upon as an evil. Economic initiative and enterprise are praised and rewarded. Social wealth, economic development as such, have come to be seen as primary social goods. This change can be connected with the central role that commerce and the profit motive have come to play in the modern, capitalist, world.[11]

In this respect, the Sophists are more in tune than Plato with the main direction that modern thinking has taken. This indicates that the Sophist position constitutes an influential and important philosophy which cannot be dismissed as mere fallacy. However, it would be a mistake to regard Plato's ideas as dead and finished. They also live on. They are at the basis of much radical criticism of the idea of progress and of modern 'affluent' consumer society.

[11] Marx, *Grundrisse*, pp. 487–8. See J. Sekora, *Luxury*, for an interesting study of these changes.

It is not clear how the happiness of different societies or different individuals can be compared; but Plato invites us to do so. A modern industrial society is immeasurably more affluent and economically developed than any in the ancient world. Routinely, we treat as necessities things which Plato could not even have imagined as possibilities. It is doubtful, however, whether all this affluence has made us any happier. The modern world is still afflicted with the problems of earlier societies – poverty, disease and ignorance – together with others of its own making.

Plato is surely right when he insists, against the Sophists, that wealth does not automatically lead to happiness; but his argument goes much further. He restricts what he considers the necessary appetites to the barest minimum. All desires above this level he regards as unnecessary. They are unnecessary for two reasons:

1. with proper education and training they need not develop; and
2. their satisfaction does us either no good or positive harm (558d–559a)

The suggestion is that these two features go together; for Plato believes that all desires beyond the minimum are both eliminable and harmful. Affluence is incompatible with individual happiness and social harmony. 'Wealth and goodness [are] like two objects in a balance, so that when one side rises the other must fall' (550e). Happiness can be achieved only if we return to a much simpler level of material existence and devote ourselves to 'higher' pursuits.

Views such as these continue to have their defenders. They are echoed in a great deal of the contemporary scepticism about the idea of progress and the benefits of economic development. Nevertheless, they are questionable, and not only from a hedonist perspective. It is true that economic development does not necessarily lead to greater happiness. But why is this? Is economic development positively detrimental to happiness, as Plato suggests? Plato believes that focusing on material well-being prevents the development of higher concerns. That is questionable. On the contrary, it is arguable that economic development provides the basis of a material surplus which is the essential precondition for higher activities.

It is wrong to see economic progress only as an impediment to genuine well-being. The problem with our current situation is not an excess of wealth, but its unequal distribution. Our social system is what Plato would classify as an oligarchy: it is divided into rich and poor, and private profit is its motive principle. In a more harmonious and justly ordered society, all our inventions and discoveries and the wealth they generate could be used not just for the profit of a few but for general human benefit and well-being.

In short, affluence cannot be equated with happiness; but nor are they completely incompatible. Plato, however, takes an excessively negative view of wealth and the appetites. In his picture of the harmonious personality, the appetites are entirely subordinated to reason. He thus extends the inequalitarianism and elitism of his account of society to his picture of the self, with similarly objectionable consequences. Just as the hierarchial and elitist aspects of his political philosophy need to be criticised, so too his picture of the individual must be rethought so that it incorporates a more equal and democratic picture of the self (cf. p. 60 above).

Concluding Thoughts

Plato rounds off his comparison of justice and injustice with a mathematical calculation designed to demonstrate that the just life involves 729 times more pleasure than the life of the tyrant (587c–588a). The significance of this passage is not well understood. It is not clear even whether it is intended seriously or whether it is what Diès calls '*une plaisanterie de mathématicien*'.[12]

In conclusion Plato summarises his moral argument with an image of the self as a composite beast of a kind familiar in Greek mythology.[13] We are to picture the personality as a creature made up of three parts. The largest part is a 'many-headed beast, with heads of wild and tame animals all round it, which it can produce and change at will' (588c). This is combined with a lion and a man. These correspond to the three parts of the self.

When we act unjustly the many-headed monster is allowed to dominate. When we are just we subject it to the ruling control of the human element, reason. The best situation is for such control

---

[12] Quoted by Lee, p. 413n.
[13] There is another image of the self as composite in *Phaedrus* 246a–b.

to be imposed from inside, by the human element within us. Failing that, it must be imposed from outside, by an external moral authority (590d).

At the beginning of the dialogue Glaucon cites the story of Gyges' ring to argue that we would all prefer to act unjustly if we could be sure to escape punishment (359c–360d). On the contrary, Plato responds, it does not ultimately benefit us to indulge our appetites and escape punishment. Acting unjustly unleashes the many-headed beast and disturbs the balance of the self. Punishment calms and tames the beast within and helps us restore inner discipline. Given what he has just said about the desirability of self-discipline, however, it is not clear why the restorative force must be imposed from outside in the form of punishment.

There is a striking finale. Glaucon asks whether the just person that Plato has been describing will take part in politics. Only in an ideal world, Plato replies, 'unless some miracle happens' (592a), for it is doubtful that anything like the perfect society which has been created in theory in the dialogue will ever exist in reality. 'It is a pattern in heaven where he who wishes can see it and found it in his own heart' (592b).

Does this support the view that Plato rejects the very idea of utopian politics, as Strauss and Bloom suggest? It would be perverse to read these words in this way. Plato has spent the whole dialogue constructing a utopian vision. He has emphasised throughout that it is an ideal and not an actually existing society. Nevertheless, as he argues in the central books of the dialogue, this vision, this ideal 'pattern', exists in thought and is of supreme importance. Only exceptionally will circumstances arise in which it can be used to guide politics in practice. More often the situation is bleaker. The ideal is dismissed and ignored by those in power and the philosopher is treated like the navigator on the ship of drunken sailors. Even in the darkest times, however, the ideal can still guide those who can grasp it in ordering their individual lives. That is the value of utopian ideas.

Guide to Further Reading

Annas, *Introduction to Plato's* Republic, Chapter 12, has a useful discussion of the issues raised in this section, in part replying to the unduly dismissive account given in Cross and Woozley, *Plato's Republic*, Chapter 11. Nettleship, *Lectures*, Chapter 14, is also helpful on the final comparison of justice and injustice, though his account of the imperfect forms of society and self (Chapter 13) is more routine. A fuller and more detailed discussion of the issues in this section can be found in T. Irwin, *Plato's Ethics*, Chapters 17 and 19.

There are other important treatments of pleasure by Plato in the *Gorgias* and *Philebus* (a difficult piece of writing). Mill repeats some of Plato's arguments in his well-known discussion of 'higher' and 'lower' pleasures in *Utilitarianism*, Chapter 2. I discuss some of the issues raised in this chapter at greater length in *Marxism and Human Nature*, Chapters 2–3. Nietzsche rejects the whole Platonic approach in an exhilaratingly sweeping fashion in *Twilight of the Idols*, and *The Birth of Tragedy*, Sections 12–15.

13 The Quarrel between Philosophy and Poetry (X.595a–608b)

The main argument of the *Republic* comes to a conclusion at the end of Book IX. Book X has the character of an appendix. It divides into two distinct and unrelated parts: the first deals with poetry and the arts (595a–608b); the second describes the rewards of justice in this life and the next (608b–621d).

The topic of poetry and the arts is introduced abruptly with a reference back to the discussion in Book III. What was said there, it is suggested, needs further justification which can now be given in terms of the tripartite theory of the self and, though it is not mentioned here, the Theory of Forms. However, the attack on poetry which ensues differs in some significant respects from anything said earlier (or in other works), particularly as regards the Theory of Forms. This has led to speculation that Book X may have been composed separately and added subsequently, but there is no direct evidence which could help to settle this question.

In any case, Plato's discussion has been enormously influential and controversial. It is sometimes said that Plato has 'no theory of art'.[1] This is misleading. As earlier, his focus is on the social and educational role of the arts, though he acknowledges that they may be considered in other lights (387c), for example, as entertainment. Nevertheless, in the course of the discussion he develops ideas about the nature and content of the arts which give this passage a claim to be the first surviving work of aesthetic theory.

[1] G. C. Field, *The Philosophy of Plato*, p. 167.

Imitation in the Arts

The central concept in Plato's account is *mimēsis*, usually translated either as 'imitation' or 'representation' (Lee, Cornford). Its meaning has elements of both. There is a marked shift in Plato's use of the term. In Book III, it denotes a particular form of poetry, namely that which uses direct speech rather than narration or description. The context is his discussion of education. Recitation of the works of Homer and other poets was a standard part of Greek schooling. Reciters or performers are engaging in 'imitation' when they directly impersonate a character in a poem or play. Plato is concerned about the moral impact of this on the young Guardians, particularly when bad or ridiculous characters are portrayed. He proposes to ban or rewrite all poetry which involves such imitation, and exclude it from the education of the young Guardians, although he allows a partial exception for cases where people of good character are being portrayed (395b–398b).

When he refers back to this passage at the beginning of Book X, he suggests that all 'imitation' has been banned. This is not the case. Moreover, it soon transpires that the term is now being used in a different sense. Earlier it denoted a particular kind of poetry, now it describes a feature of all poetry and, indeed, all (realistic) art whatever: that it 'imitates', 'represents', pictures or copies nature. And his concern now is for the moral impact of such art on the audience rather than on the performer. There is no mention of such discrepancies. Plato launches into a vigorous attack on the arts in so far as they are regarded as representing reality: they give no knowledge of the world, and they have harmful effects on their audience. Except for hymns to the gods and poems in praise of good people, imitative art is banned from the ideal society (607a).

The Attack on Poetry

Plato explains the concept of artistic imitation (*mimēsis*) in the terms of the Theory of Forms, using the example of painting. A picture of a bed is a two-dimensional representation not of the three-dimensional object, but only of the way it appears from a particular angle. The bed itself, moreover, is only a particular sensible object, only one of the many particular examples of the single Form of bed. Thus three 'sorts of beds' (597b) are involved here: the Form of the bed, a particular material bed and its painted image.[2] Corresponding to these there are three different kinds of making (*poiēsis*). The Form is made by god; the physical bed is made by a carpenter who imitates or copies the Form or ideal; and the image is made by a painter who reproduces the appearance of the bed. The painted image is thus twice removed from reality and truth (597e).

It is difficult to reconcile some of this with what Plato says earlier (and elsewhere) about the Theory of Forms. The idea that Forms are created by god cannot be reconciled with Plato's usual view that they are eternal and hence uncreated. Nor is it clear how a carpenter's work can be guided by a knowledge of the Form when only philosophers are supposed to have such knowledge. Moreover, Plato does not usually hold that there are Forms for humanly created objects such as beds.

Putting these problems aside, however, Plato's basic point is clear enough. Painting is a mindless and mechanical copying of immediate appearances which are remote from reality and truth. Poetry is similar, he now argues. It paints a picture in words as it were. Although it seems able to tell us about any and every topic, in reality it conveys no genuine knowledge: it deals only with superficial appearances. Like painting, it creates only an image of an appearance. Plato concentrates his attack on Homer, the greatest and most revered Greek poet. His work is far distant from reality or truth. It conveys no genuine knowledge of human nature or human affairs. 'All the poets from Homer downwards have no grasp of truth but merely produce a superficial likeness of any subject they treat' (600e).

Plato supports this indictment with a further brief argument which draws on his earlier account of knowledge. There are three different ways in which an object may be known. Plato gives the example of a flute. The player who uses it has the greatest knowledge; the craftsman who makes it must have correct opinions about it, based on the reports of the flute player; whereas the artist needs neither knowledge nor correct opinion of the flute,

---

[2] It is better to regard these as three different ways in which a bed can be present to us, cf. p. 112 above.

but only an acquaintance with its appearance, in order to portray it in a convincing fashion which will satisfy the 'ignorant multitude'. The suggestion is that mimetic art embodies only the lowest sort of knowledge, the illusion (*eikasia*) of the lowest segment of the Divided Line. 'The artist knows little or nothing about the subjects he represents and ... the art of representation is something that has no serious value ... this applies above all to all tragic poetry, epic or dramatic' (602b).

Plato is equally critical of the moral and psychological effects of poetry. It appeals to the lowest part of the self, to the emotions and not to reason. Again he uses visual cases to make his point. The example so beloved of philosophers – the stick which appears bent when half emersed in water – makes its first appearance here. Illusions of this sort are detected and corrected by the use of reason which 'calculates' and 'measures' (602d). They arise when the influence of the lower part of the self, the senses, prevails.

Something similar is true with poetry which creates what Plato treats as emotional illusions. Poetry stirs up our emotions while, at the same time, relaxing the control of the rational part of the self. In everyday life the emotions are generally under the control of the higher, rational part of the self; but such restraint lacks dramatic interest. So the poet is led to show characters indulging their emotions without the usual restraint. The effects of poetry are corrupting and harmful and this is 'the gravest charge' against it (605c).

The Ancient Quarrel

Plato's attack on the arts seems crude and exaggerated. It becomes somewhat more comprehensible when seen in context. Poetry had a place in ancient Greek life quite different from that which it has today. The culture was predominantly oral. Memorising and reciting verse was still the main vehicle for education and the transmission of ideas and attitudes. The words of the poets and tragedians were cited as authoritative on moral and social questions and for general guidance on many other topics (as for example by Polemarchus in Book I). Homer was revered above all as 'the educator of Greece' (606e). Plato's attack is aimed specifically at these claims. His critique of poetry and drama is made in the name of philosophy. Genuine knowledge, he is arguing, comes from the exercise of reason – from philosophy in a broad sense – rather than from literature and the arts.

To some extent the point that Plato is making is so much taken for granted in the modern world that there is a danger of missing its significance. No doubt, many of our ideas about the human world still come to us via literature and drama (including now, of course, TV, film, etc.). However, ethics, politics, history, psychology, sociology and other subjects are well established as branches of knowledge; and it is to these that we turn for systematic understanding in these areas. The arts no longer have the authority as a source of knowledge that Plato is questioning.

Plato's ideas are a part of the wider intellectual movement which makes up the Greek enlightenment and which results in the birth of philosophy. For the first time the traditional culture, and the central place of literature in it, was being challenged. Thinkers, including the Sophists and Socrates, were attempting to understand and explain the world in rational terms. Plato is a leading figure in this movement. Although his moral and social attitudes are very conservative, he attempts to justify them in rational terms. Supporting philosophy in what he terms its ancient 'quarrel' with poetry is a central concern for him (607b). The defence of philosophy against rhetoric and the arts (which he treats as a sort of rhetoric) is a major theme in all his work.

Poetry and Philosophy

The historical context goes some way towards explaining Plato's attitude to poetry and the sharp contrast he draws between it and philosophy; but it does not answer the criticism that his account of it as the mere copying of outward appearances is crude and unsatisfactory. Moreover, the sharp distinction he draws between poetry and philosophy seems equally simplistic, and leads to a false picture of both.

Plato himself seems to have come to realise this; his views on these topics develop significantly through the course of his work. In his writings up to and including the *Republic* a polemical purpose seems to dominate. Poetry is classed as a sort of rhetoric and sharply opposed to philosophy. Both rhetoric and poetry are treated in an extremely hostile and dismissive fashion. They involve uses of language which appeal to the emotions rather than reason for their effects; in contrast to philosophy they convey no knowledge.[3]

A more nuanced and complex approach emerges in the *Phaedrus*, a later dialogue. Instead of dismissing all rhetoric and poetry as deceptive and harmful, Plato allows that there can be good as well as bad rhetoric, good as well as bad poetry. Good rhetoric – rhetoric which is genuinely persuasive – embodies knowledge of its topic; it approaches to philosophy. Good poetry, similarly, embodies knowledge.[4]

The sharp contrast between poetry and philosophy that runs through Plato's early dialogues is also criticised by Aristotle. In a passage in the *Poetics* which is thought to be a direct response to this section of the *Republic*, Aristotle maintains that poetry is more philosophical than Plato suggests. Unlike history, poetry does not simply record the particular actions of particular individuals. It is concerned with 'types of persons' and the 'kinds of things' they may do in a given situation. It is not primarily concerned with what actually occurred, but with what is 'probable or necessary'. Thus there is a 'philosophical' dimension to poetry, it is 'concerned with universals and not just particular facts'.[5]

Aristotle is surely right about this. Indeed, the point he is making is implicitly recognised by Plato elsewhere in the *Republic*, where his main worry is about the general moral influence of poetry and the false ideas it conveys about the gods and human nature.

Philosophy and Poetry

If Plato's denial that poetry embodies knowledge is questionable, so too is his account of philosophy as a purely rational pursuit. Philosophy is never that; it is always expressed in language which involves a rhetorical and literary element. This is particularly evident in Plato's own dialogues, many of which are masterpieces

---

[3] This view is most fully set out in the *Gorgias*.

[4] The theoretical possibility of good rhetoric is recognised in the *Gorgias*, but its existence in practice is discounted (503), perhaps because this would cut across the polemical purpose of this work.

[5] Aristotle, *Poetics* 1451a–b. Aristotle's view that history is a mere chronicle of facts is questionable, but that is not relevant here.

of literature as well as philosophy, and in which the literary devices of metaphor, simile, allegory and myth are frequently employed with great skill to communicate a philosophical message.

Sometimes the use of such literary devices is regarded as a feature only of a specifically 'literary' style of philosophical writing, which in recent years has been associated particularly with 'continental' philosophy. This is then contrasted unfavourably with the 'plain' and 'straightforward' style of 'analytic' philosophers in the English-speaking world. Thus the ancient quarrel between philosophy and literature is continued into the present-day.

The attempt to draw a sharp distinction between philosophy and literature in this Platonic fashion is untenable. Philosophy is always expressed and communicated in a persuasive fashion, whatever its style (though of course this may be done well or badly). There is a literary and rhetorical aspect to *all* writing. This is as true of the plainest and most formal analytical writing as it is of the most florid 'literary' prose. Indeed, an austere and formal style is itself one of the rhetorical devices of analytical philosophy. In short, there is both a philosophical dimension to literature and a literary dimension to philosophy. The two cannot be distinguished in the categorical manner suggested by Plato in the *Republic*.

This is not to deny that there are fundamental differences between the two along the lines that Plato indicates. For Plato is right to maintain that poetry and art work through the particular. The universals they express are always embodied in a concrete and individual form, in specific characters, incidents and images. Although poetry and drama may describe human action in terms that are informed by an understanding of the principles of human psychology and human nature, this understanding remains implicit. It is not formulated as such. Poets do not 'give an account' of these principles. They cannot explain their own works, says Plato. These are products of irrational 'inspiration' (*mania*) not of wisdom.[6] For explicitly formulated knowledge we must turn to rational disciplines like philosophy or psychology.

According to the Platonic view, the claim that philosophy is a higher form of knowledge than poetry is justified on this basis.

---

[6] *Apology* 21–2. See also *Phaedrus* on the role of inspiration in poetry and philosophy. For Plato it is a characteristic feature of knowledge that it can 'give an account', *Gorgias* 501; cf. *Meno* 97–8.

Philosophy makes explicit what remains only implicit and unarticulated in poetry. In philosophy, moreover, the highest reality, the universal form, is dealt with directly and not merely via particulars. Knowledge is thus freed from its connections with what is merely concrete and individual and considered by and in itself.

However, these matters can be looked at in a quite different way. 'Life is green but theory is grey', says Goethe. By portraying the universal as embodied in the particular, art sees things concretely. It captures the richness of the real world, while philosophy is abstract and etiolated. A more balanced and satisfactory view than Plato's is that both philosophy and poetry are valid forms of representation. Both embody genuine forms of knowledge and are complementary, not competing, expressions of the human spirit.

By demanding that poetry should convey knowledge it is sometimes said that Plato is judging poetry by the standards of philosophy and thus initiating what Danto calls the 'philosophical disenfranchisement of art'. Plato's philosophy can be defended against this charge. One of its most enduring aspects is the view that art has a realistic content: it represents reality and can be assessed in these terms. This is not its only function or the only criterion for its assessment – art also arouses the emotions, entertains, etc. On the Platonic view, however, the representation of reality is an essential and fundamental purpose of serious art. To insist on this is not necessarily to subordinate art to philosophy. For we should acknowledge, as Plato does not, that art and philosophy involve different but equally valid ways in which reality can be represented and knowledge conveyed. The ancient quarrel between them must be transcended.

Art and the Emotions

Plato's account of the emotional effects of the arts also raises controversial and difficult questions. He sees them as having a psychologically damaging effect: provoking the emotions, inhibiting the rational part of the self, and thus disturbing its balance.[7]

---

[7] This passage also raises issues about control and censorship of the arts which are discussed in Ch. 4 above.

This may sometimes occur but, again, Plato's views seem crude and simplistic. They seem motivated as much by a desire to denigrate the arts as to understand them. Again there is a more complex and satisfactory account in the *Phaedrus*, which recognises the 'charm' that literature exerts and that this can be used either for good or for evil.

Plato's account in the *Republic* is interestingly criticised in Aristotle's *Poetics*. Aristotle agrees that tragic poetry provokes strong emotions of 'fear and pity'. However, he maintains that the feelings which are engendered by tragedy are at the same time released and purged by it. Thus tragedy involves a sort of purging of emotion or *katharsis*. By helping us to deal with these emotions it is psychologically beneficial not harmful.

It is unlikely that either Plato or Aristotle has the whole truth here. It seems rather that some works of art have the effect described by Plato and others that described by Aristotle. There are other alternatives as well. The arts can stimulate the imagination, widen experience, delight and charm, etc. However, these aspects are beyond the scope of Plato's discussion. He does not pretend to give a full theory of art. His purpose is limited and polemical. Even so, the *Republic* is one of the first works in which the nature and impact of art is thought about in philosophical terms. And crude and inadequate as some of his formulations may be, he raises many of the issues which have been central to the philosophy of art ever since.

Guide to Further Reading

This is one of the most influential and controversial sections in the whole dialogue. It has provoked a huge literature. There are good general accounts in Crombie, *Examination of Plato's Doctrines*, Volume I, Chapter 3 Section 7 and Chapter 5; C. Janaway, *Images of Excellence: Plato's Critique of the Arts*, Chapters 5, 6 and 8; and J. O. Urmson, 'Plato and the Poets'.

Other important discussions of poetry by Plato can be found in the *Gorgias, Phaedrus* and *Laws*, Book II. G. R. F. Ferrari, 'Plato and Poetry', and Grube, *Plato's Thought*, Chapter 6, survey the development of Plato's views on art through all his work.

Influential discussions of the philosophical issues raised by these are in Aristotle, *Poetics*, and Hegel, *Introduction to Aesthetics*. The critique of the Platonic approach in Nietzsche, *Birth of Tragedy*, Sections 12–15, has had a huge impact on contemporary thought, some of which is traced in C. H. Zuckert, *Postmodern Platos*.

E. A. Havelock, *Preface to Plato*, contains a fascinating though controversial account of the historical context of Plato's attack on poetry. On the ancient 'quarrel' between philosophy and poetry, see M. C. Nussbaum, *The Fragility of Goodness*, Chapter 1. For the recent quarrel on this topic between analytical and continental philosophy see J. Derrida, 'Signature Event Context'; R. Rorty, 'Deconstruction and Circumvention'; and C. Norris, *Derrida*, Chapter 2.

How Plato's own use of poetical devices can be reconciled with his attack on poetry is discussed in Nussbaum, *The Fragility of Goodness*, pp. 122–35, and Ferrari, 'Plato and Poetry', pp. 141–8.

14 The Rewards of Justice
(X.608c–621d)

At the end Plato returns to the theme with which he began: our reasons for being just. The dialogue concludes with an account of the afterlife, told in the form of a myth. From a philosophical point of view this section is disappointing. It divides into three distinct parts dealing with:

1. arguments for immortality (608c–612a);
2. the rewards of justice in this life (612a–614a); and
3. after death as recounted in the Myth of Er (614a–end)

The Immortality of the Soul (608c–612a)

Plato's commitment to the doctrine of the immortality of the soul cannot be doubted. It features in other dialogues, notably the *Phaedo* which describes Socrates' final hours and his attitude to death and in which it is argued for at length. In the *Republic*, unfortunately, the arguments for it are perfunctory and weak.

The topic is introduced abruptly. The benefits of justice, Socrates asserts, are much greater than so far supposed. They must be counted not just in this life but in the next as well. When Glaucon expresses surprise at this sudden talk of an afterlife, he is assured that to prove the immortality of the soul (*psuchē*) is 'nothing difficult' (608d).[1]

Every thing has its own specific good which improves and preserves it, and its own specific evil which corrupts and destroys

---

[1] I use the term 'soul' in this section rather than 'self' since we have moved onto spiritual terrain.

it. Nothing else can do so. Injustice is the soul's specific evil. The specific evils of the body, such as disease, though they may lead to the death of the body, cannot affect the soul. The only sort of evil that affects the self is moral. Yet this is not fatal to the self; even the most unjust person is still a person. Hence nothing can destroy the soul, it is immortal. Plato also maintains that the number of souls is always constant, laying the ground for his belief in reincarnation.

As a proof this is scarcely compelling. It relies on a number of dubious and unsupported assumptions. In the first place, it assumes that things have only a single particular 'evil' and, specifically, that only injustice can harm the soul. But most things, it seems, face a variety of evils. Arguably the soul can be deranged and even destroyed by a whole range of adverse circumstances, psychological and material. Plato denies this. He assumes that soul and body are entirely separate, each with its own particular evil, so that what kills the body does not destroy the soul. This is the main point that needs to be established if the argument for immortality is to get off the ground. It cannot simply be presupposed at the outset.

Moreover, it conflicts with the account that Plato has given of the self. Plato himself is aware of this problem. He holds that whatever is composed of parts can, and ultimately will, be altered and destroyed – an immortal entity must be simple. This cannot be reconciled with the theory that the self has three parts which is the basis for the account of justice in the rest of the dialogue.

The solution that Plato now adopts creates more problems than it solves. The tripartite self is only the everyday self which is 'deformed by its association with the body and other evils' (611c). The true character of the soul is hidden. Plato likens it to the sea god Glaucus, whose human form is covered over with barnacles and seaweed through long immersion in the ocean depths. The soul's 'true nature', Plato says, can be glimpsed from its rational part, which aspires to and resembles what is 'divine, immortal and eternal' (611e).

This is a striking image but it does not constitute a valid argument. Moreover, it has drastic implications. It treats the appetites and desires as alien to the true self – the immortal self – which is now identified with the rational part only. I have already drawn attention to Plato's ambivalent attitude to the appetites (p. 142–3 above). Here, however, they are entirely excluded from the self. In effect Plato thus discards the earlier account of the three parts of the soul as a superficial appearance.

If we must choose between the earlier account of the self as a complex entity and the doctrine of immortality as expounded here, then the dialogue as a whole surely shows that the former has more going for it. The true lesson of the *Republic* is not that we should slough off the encrustation of our bodily being in favour of a life of pure reason, but that our bodily appetites are part of our true nature too, and happiness can come only from the harmonious satisfaction of all parts of the personality.

The Rewards of Justice in this Life (612a–614a)

The discussion now switches suddenly to the rewards of justice in this life. Such earthly preoccupations sit awkwardly with the focus on immortality in the previous passage. Nevertheless, the overall line of thought is clear enough. Since the soul is immortal, Plato is arguing, the benefits of justice must be counted both in this world and in the next.

In the main argument of Books II–IX Plato's aim is to demonstrate that justice is good in itself, and that we should be just even if we have Gyges' ring and have no fear of being detected if we behave wrongly. For the purposes of the main argument the consequences which follow from being just were set aside. A complete picture of justice must take them into account. Plato now asserts that justice is honoured both by humans and the gods, and it is generally rewarded in the end. Thrasymachus was wrong to maintain that it pays to be unjust. Glaucon and Adeimantus' worries on this score are unfounded.

No argument is given in support of these bland assurances. If they are true then Socrates could have used them to respond to Thrasymachus, Glaucon and Adeimantus at the start and everyone could have gone home a lot earlier. Plato seems to have forgotten the fate of Socrates and the bitter but surely more realistic picture of the predicament of the philosopher in an unjust society in Book VI.

Even if it is true that justice is generally rewarded, Annas questions whether Plato should be praising it in this way.[2] The

---

[2] Annas, *Introduction to Plato's* Republic, pp. 349–50.

main argument defends justice as an inner state of the self, desirable in itself and not because it is externally rewarded. Plato's view, it sometimes seems, is that external rewards are irrelevant.

In fact this is not so. At the outset all agree that justice is desirable both in itself and for its consequences. This view is maintained throughout, and the final section is consistent with it. The impression that Plato cares nothing for external rewards is created by his hostile attitude to the appetites. However, to reiterate the point just made, Plato is most fruitfully read, not as an ascetic thinker but as one who allows the appetites an essential role in the self. This implies that some level of material prosperity and reputation is necessary for happiness.[3]

The issue of the rewards is relevant, then. Though it is not the primary reason to be just, nevertheless we strongly feel that justice should be rewarded. According to Plato, however, justice is defined as a state of inner harmony, and there seems no necessary connection between this and external rewards. How can we be sure that Thrasymachus is wrong and that it pays to be just? There is a deep problem here, but unfortunately Plato has nothing interesting to say about it in this brief section. Kant is much exercised by it. He concludes that we can have no proof that justice leads to happiness but only 'faith' in 'providence' to which we are led by reason, the conviction that the order of the universe is ultimately rational and good.[4] I cannot help but think that Plato would have welcomed these views as an extension of his own.

The Myth of Er

Justice is also rewarded in the hereafter. The dialogue ends with a picture of life after death in the poetical form of a myth. This comes strangely after Plato's attack on poetry. Yet Plato often resorts to myth in his dialogues, and the *Phaedo* and *Gorgias* end similarly.

These myths play a distinctive role in Plato's writing. In them he expresses ideas and deals with issues which are beyond the

---

[3] This is better appreciated by Aristotle who has an altogether more materialistic and securely embodied conception of the self (*Ethics* 1099a). For a contrasting account which emphasises Plato's asceticism, see Nussbaum, *The Fragility of Goodness*, Ch. 5.

[4] Kant, *Critique of Teleological Judgement*, Sections 26–8.

scope of rational and scientific demonstration, but which are inescapably presented by the enquiry in hand. Because Plato leaves us in no doubt about the mythical status of such stories, we are 'inoculated' against their dangers (595b).

Kant accuses Plato of what he calls the 'transcendent' use, or rather misuse, of reason: that is, of speculating about matters such as immortality beyond the limits of any possible knowledge.

> The light dove, cleaving the air in her free flight and feeling its resistance, might imagine that its flight would be still easier in empty space. It was thus that Plato left the world of the senses, as setting too narrow limits to the understanding, and ventured out beyond it on the wings of the ideas, in the empty space of the pure understanding. He did not observe that, with all his efforts, he made no advance – meeting no resistance that might, as it were, serve as a support upon which he could take a stand.[5]

Plato may at times be guilty as charged, but not in this passage. By presenting his ideas explicitly in the form of myth, he clearly distinguishes them from the reasoned argument which comprises the main substance of his philosophy and does not claim the status of knowledge for them.[6]

The myth takes the form of a story told by the warrior Er who is killed in battle but returns to life after twelve days in the next world. It divides into two parts. In the first, Er describes the judgement of souls. The just are rewarded, the evil are punished in a sort of purgatory. Most are eventually reincarnated; only a few incurably evil souls are damned eternally. There is no suggestion that the just can escape from the cycle of reincarnation in an eternal heaven.

The second part concerns the processes leading up to reincarnation. Plato outlines a cosmological theory. The details are complex and not of concern here. An important aspect of the story conveys Plato's ideas of free will and necessity. Unlike the fatalistic Hindu notion of *karma*, in Plato's story the soul itself chooses the life into which it will be reborn, though the choice is influenced by its previous character. Then the life is lived out in circumstances necessarily determined. Whether or not we are

---

[5] Kant, *Critique of Pure Reason*, p. 47 (A5 = B9).
[6] In this respect such mythically presented ideas are similar to Kant's 'ideas' of reason, which include God and Immortality.

virtuous is in our hands: the responsibility lies 'not with god, but with the soul that makes the choice' (617e).

Guide to Further Reading

Crombie, *Examination of Plato's Doctrines*, Volume I, pp. 150–1, and Nettleship, *Lectures*, Chapter 16, give helpful accounts of this section, which is of relatively minor philosophical interest.

Grube, *Plato's Thought*, Chapter 4, gives a general account of Plato's views on the soul. J. A. Stewart, *The Myths of Plato*, is still suggestive on the role of myth in Plato's writings, as well as giving a detailed commentary on the Myth of Er.

Bibliography

The following bibliography includes a selection of introductory works as well as material cited in the text. It is arranged according to subject.

Plato *Collected Dialogues*, ed. E. Hamilton and H. Cairns. Princeton: Princeton University Press, 1961.

Plato *Gorgias*, trans. Walter Hamilton. Harmondsworth: Penguin, rev. edn, 1971.

Plato *The Last Days of Socrates: Euthyphro, The Apology, Crito, Phaedo*, trans. Hugh Tredennick. Harmondsworth: Penguin, rev. edn, 1969.

Plato *The Laws*, trans. Trevor J. Saunders. Harmondsworth: Penguin, 1970.

Plato *Phaedrus and Letters VII and VIII*, trans. W. Hamilton. Harmondsworth: Penguin, 1973.

Plato *Protagoras and Meno*, trans. W. K. C. Guthrie. Harmondsworth: Penguin, 1956.

Plato *The Republic*, trans. F. M. Cornford. London: Oxford University Press, 1941.

Plato *The Republic*, trans. H. D. P. Lee. Harmondsworth: Penguin, 2nd rev. edn, 1987.

Plato *The Symposium*, trans. W. Hamilton. Harmondsworth: Penguin, 1951.

Plato *Theaetetus*. In *Plato's Theory of Knowledge*, trans. F. M. Cornford. London: Routledge & Kegan Paul, 1935.

Life and Background

Andrewes, A. *Greek Society.* Harmondsworth: Penguin, 1971.

Burn, A. R. *The Pelican History of Greece.* Harmondsworth: Penguin, 1966.

de Ste. Croix, G. E. M. *The Class Struggle in the Ancient Greek World: From the Archaic Age to the Arab Conquests.* London: Duckworth, 1981.

Dodds, E. R. *The Greeks and the Irrational.* Boston: Beacon Press, 1957.

Dover, K. J. *Greek Homosexuality.* London: Duckworth, 1978.

Jones, A. H. M. *Athenian Democracy.* Oxford: Blackwell, paperback edn, 1977.

Kitto, H. D. F. *The Greeks.* Harmondsworth: Penguin, 1951.

Wood, E. M., and Wood, N. *Class Ideology and Ancient Political Theory: Socrates, Plato, and Aristotle in Social Context.* Oxford: Blackwell, 1978.

Commentaries and General Works

Annas, J. *An Introduction to Plato's* Republic. Oxford: Clarendon Press, 1981.

Bloom, A. 'Interpretive Essay'. In *The* Republic *of Plato.* New York: Basic Books, 1968, 307–436.

Bosanquet, B. *A Companion to Plato's* Republic *for English Readers.* London: Rivington, Percival & Co., 2nd edn, 1895.

Cornford, F. M. *Before and after Socrates.* Cambridge: Cambridge University Press, 1932.

Crombie, I. M. *An Examination of Plato's Doctrines*, Vol. I, *Plato on Man and Society.* London: Routledge & Kegan Paul, 1962.

Cross, R. C., and Woozley, A. D. *Plato's* Republic*: A Philosophical Commentary.* London: Macmillan, 1964.

Field, G. C. *The Philosophy of Plato.* London: Oxford University Press, 1949.

Gosling, J. C. *Plato.* London: Routledge & Kegan Paul, 1973.

Grote, G. *Plato, and the Other Companions of Sokrates* (3 Vols). London: John Murray, 1865, Vol. III, Chs 33–5.

Grube, G. M. A. *Plato's Thought.* London: Methuen, 1935.

Guthrie, W. K. C. *A History of Greek Philosophy*, Vol. IV. Cambridge: Cambridge University Press, 1975.

Hegel, G. W. F. *Lectures on the History of Philosophy* (3 Vols), trans. E. S. Haldane and Frances H. Simson. London: Routledge & Kegan Paul, 1892, Vol. II, Ch. IIIA.

MacIntyre, A. *A Short History of Ethics*. London: Routledge & Kegan Paul, 1967.

Nettleship, R. L. *Lectures on the* Republic *of Plato*. London: Macmillan, 2nd edn, 1901.

Nussbaum, M. C. *The Fragility of Goodness: Luck and Ethics in Greek Tragedy and Philosophy*. Cambridge: Cambridge University Press, 1986.

Pappas, N. *Plato and the* Republic. London: Routledge, 1995.

Sesonske, A. (ed.) *Plato's* Republic*: Interpretation and Criticism*. Belmont, CA: Wadsworth, 1966.

Taylor, A. E. *Plato: The Man and His Work*. London: Methuen, 1926.

Vlastos, G. (ed.) *Plato: A Collection of Critical Essays* (2 Vols). Garden City, NY: Anchor Books, 1971.

Vlastos, G. *Platonic Studies*. Princeton: Princeton University Press, 2nd edn, 1981.

White, N. P. *A Companion to Plato's* Republic. Indianapolis: Hackett, 1979.

Zuckert, C. H. *Postmodern Platos: Nietzsche, Heidegger, Gadamer, Strauss, Derrida*. Chicago: University of Chicago Press, 1996.

Social and Political Thought

Bambrough, J. R. (ed.) *Plato, Popper and Politics*. Cambridge: Heffer, 1967.

Barker, E. *Greek Political Theory: Plato and His Predecessors*. London: Methuen, 5th edn, 1960.

Barker, E. *The Political Thought of Plato and Aristotle*. New York: Dover, 1959.

Bloom, A. 'Response to Hall'. *Political Theory* 5, No. 3 (1977), 315–330.

Crossman, R. H. S. *Plato Today*. London: Allen & Unwin, rev. 2nd edn, 1959.

Foster, M. B. *The Political Philosophies of Plato and Hegel*. Oxford: Clarendon Press, 1935.

Gouldner, A. W. *Enter Plato: Classical Greece and the Origins of Social Theory*. London: Routledge & Kegan Paul, 1967.

Hall, D. 'The *Republic* and the "Limits of Politics"'. *Political Theory* 5, No. 3 (1977), 293–313.

Havelock, E. A. *The Greek Concept of Justice*. Cambridge, MA: Harvard University Press, 1978.

Klosko, G. 'The "Straussian" Interpretation of Plato's *Republic*'. *History of Political Thought* 7, No. 2 (1986), 275–93.

Leys, W. A. R. 'Was Plato Non-Political?' In G. Vlastos (ed.), *Plato*, Vol. II. Garden City, NY: Anchor Books, 1971, 166–173.

Neu, J. 'Plato's Analogy of State and Individual: The *Republic* and the Organic Theory of the State'. *Philosophy* 46 (1971), 238–54.

Popper, K. R. *The Open Society and Its Enemies*, Vol. I, *The Spell of Plato*. London: Routledge & Kegan Paul, 5th edn, 1966.

Sparshott, F. E. 'Plato as Anti-Political Thinker'. In G. Vlastos (ed.), *Plato*, Vol. II. Garden City, NY: Anchor Books, 1971, 174–83.

Stalley, R. F. 'Aristotle's Criticism of Plato's *Republic*'. In D. Keyt and F. D. Miller (eds), *A Companion to Aristotle's Politics*. Oxford: Blackwell, 1991, 182–99.

Strauss, L. *The City and Man*. Chicago: Rand McNally & Co., 1964, Ch. 2.

Versenyi, L. G. 'Plato and His Liberal Opponents'. *Philosophy* 46 (1971), 222–37.

Vlastos, G. 'Does Slavery Exist in Plato's *Republic*?' *Classical Philology* 63 (1968), 291–5.

Vlastos, G. 'Slavery in Plato's Thought'. *Philosophical Review* 50 (1941), 289–304.

Williams, B. 'The Analogy of City and Soul in Plato's *Republic*'. In E. N. Lee, A. P. D. Mourelatos and R. M. Rorty (eds), *Exegesis and Argument*. Assen: Van Gorcum, 1973, 196–206.

Wolin, S. S. *Politics and Vision: Continuity and Innovation in Western Political Thought*. Boston: Little, Brown and Co., 1960, Ch. 2.

Women and the Family

Annas, J. 'Plato's *Republic* and Feminism'. *Philosophy* 51 (1976), 307–21.

Calvert, B. 'Plato and the Equality of Women'. *Phoenix* 29 (1975), 231–43.

Coole, D. H. *Women in Political Theory: From Ancient Misogyny to Contemporary Feminism*. Hemel Hempstead: Harvester-Wheatsheaf, 2nd edn, 1993.

Elshtain, J. B. *Public Man, Private Woman: Women in Social and Political Thought*. Princeton: Princeton University Press, 2nd edn, 1993.

Fortenbaugh, W. 'Plato, Temperament and Eugenic Policy'. *Arethusa* 8, No. 2 (1975), 283–306.

Lesser, H. 'Plato's Feminism'. *Philosophy* 54 (1979), 113–17.

Mulhern, J. J. 'Population and Plato's *Republic*'. *Arethusa* 8, No. 2 (1975), 265–81.

Okin, S. M. 'Philosopher Queens and Private Wives: Plato on Women and the Family'. *Philosophy and Public Affairs* 6, No. 4 (1977), 345–69.

Pierce, C. 'Equality: *Republic* V'. *The Monist* 57, No. 1 (1973), 1–11.

Moral Philosophy

Demos, R. 'A Fallacy in Plato's *Republic*?. In G. Vlastos (ed.), *Plato*, Vol. II. Garden City, NY: Anchor Books, 1971, 52–6.

Foster, M. B. 'A Mistake in Plato's *Republic*'. *Mind* 46 (1937), 386–93.

Henderson, T. Y. 'In Defence of Thrasymachus'. *American Philosophical Quarterly* 7 (1970), 218–28.

Irwin, T. *Plato's Ethics*. New York: Oxford University Press, 1995.

Joseph, H. W. B. 'Plato's *Republic*: The Argument with Polemarchus'. In A. Sesonske (ed.), *Plato's* Republic: *Interpretation and Criticism*. Belmont, CA: Wadsworth, 1966, 6–16.

Kenny, A. J. P. 'Mental Health in Plato's *Republic*'. In *The Anatomy of the Soul*. Oxford: Blackwell, 1973, 1–27.

Kraut, R. 'Reason and Justice in Plato's *Republic*'. In E. N. Lee, A. P. D. Mourelatos and R. M. Rorty (eds), *Exegesis and Argument*. Assen: Van Gorcum, 1973, 207–24.

Mabbott, J. D. 'Is Plato's *Republic* Utilitarian?'. In G. Vlastos (ed.), *Plato*, Vol. II. Garden City, NY: Anchor Books, 1971, 57–65.

Nettleship, R. L. *The Theory of Education in Plato's* Republic. London: Oxford University Press, 1935.

Norman, R. *The Moral Philosophers*. Oxford: Clarendon Press, 1983, Ch. 2.

Prichard, H. A. *Moral Obligation and Duty and Interest*. Oxford: Oxford University Press, 1968.

Sachs, D. 'A Fallacy in Plato's *Republic*'. In G. Vlastos (ed.), *Plato*, Vol. II. Garden City, NY: Anchor Books, 1971, 35–51.

Sartorius, R. 'Fallacy and Political Radicalism in Plato's *Republic*'. *Canadian Journal of Philosophy* 3 (1974), 349–63.

Vlastos, G. 'Justice and Happiness in the *Republic*'. In G. Vlastos (ed.), *Plato*, Vol. II. Garden City, NY: Anchor Books, 1971, 66–95.

Weingartner, R. 'Vulgar Justice and Platonic Justice'. *Philosophy and Phenomenological Research* 25 (1964), 248–52.

Epistemology, Metaphysics and Logic

Allen, R. E. 'Participation and Predication in Plato's Middle Dialogues'. In G. Vlastos (ed.), *Plato*, Vol. I. Garden City, NY: Anchor Books, 1971, 167–83.

Cherniss, H. F. 'The Philosophical Economy of the Theory of Ideas'. In G. Vlastos (ed.), *Plato*, Vol. I. Garden City, NY: Anchor Books, 1971, 16–27.

Crombie, I. M. *An Examination of Plato's Doctrines*, Vol. II, *Plato on Knowledge and Reality*. London: Routledge & Kegan Paul, 1963.

Crombie, I. M. *Plato: The Midwife's Apprentice*. London: Routledge & Kegan Paul, 1964.

Gadamer, H.-G. 'Hegel and the Dialectic of the Ancient Philosophers'. In *Hegel's Dialectic*. New Haven: Yale University Press, 1976, 5–34.

Heidegger, M. *Nietzsche*, Vol. I, *The Will to Power as Art*, trans. David Farrell Krell. London: Routledge & Kegan Paul, 1981.

Heidegger, M. 'Plato's Doctrine of the Truth'. In W. Barrett and H. D. Aiken (eds), *Philosophy in the Twentieth Century*, Vol. III. New York: Random House, 1962, 251–70.

Joseph, H. W. B. *Knowledge and the Good in Plato's* Republic. London: Oxford University Press, 1948.

Nehamas, A. 'Plato on the Imperfections of the Sensible World'. *American Philosophical Quarterly* 12 (1975), 105–17.

Robinson, R. 'Hypothesis in the *Republic*'. In G. Vlastos (ed.), *Plato*, Vol. I. Garden City, NY: Anchor Books, 1971, 97–131. (Reprinted from *Plato's Early Dialectic*. London: Clarendon Press, 1953, Ch. 10).

Ross, W. D. *Plato's Theory of Ideas*. Oxford: Clarendon Press, 1951.

Vlastos, G. 'Degrees of Reality in Plato'. In *Platonic Studies*. Princeton: Princeton University Press, 1965, 58–75.

Wedberg, A. 'The Theory of Ideas'. In G. Vlastos (ed.), *Plato*, Vol. I. Garden City, NY: Anchor Books, 1971, 28–52.

Wilson, J. R. S. 'The Contents of the Cave'. *Canadian Journal of Philosophy* Supplementary Vol. II (1976), 117–27.

Literature and Art

Annas, J. 'Plato on the Triviality of Literature'. In J. Moravcsik and P. Temko (eds), *Plato on Beauty, Wisdom and the Arts*. Totowa, NJ: Rowman and Littlefield, 1982, 1–28.

Beardsley, M. C. *Aesthetics from Classical Greece to the Present: A Short History*. Alabama: The University of Alabama Press, paperback edn, 1975.

Burnyeat, M. F. 'Art and Mimesis in Plato's "Republic"'. *London Review of Books* 20, No. 10 (1998), 3–9.

Collingwood, R. G. *The Principles of Art*. Oxford: Clarendon Press, 1938.

Danto, A. C. *The Philosophical Disenfranchisement of Art*. New York: Columbia University Press, 1986.

Gadamer, H.-G. 'Plato and the Poets'. In *Dialogue and Dialectic*. New Haven, CT: Yale University Press, 1980, 39–72.

Havelock, E. A. *Preface to Plato*. Oxford: Blackwell, 1963.

Janaway, C. *Images of Excellence: Plato's Critique of the Arts*. Oxford: Clarendon Press, 1995.

Moravcsik, J., and Temko, P. (eds) *Plato on Beauty, Wisdom and the Arts*. Totowa, NJ: Rowman and Littlefield, 1982.

Murdoch, I. *The Fire and the Sun: Why Plato Banished the Artists*. Oxford: Clarendon Press, 1977.

Nehamas, A. 'Plato on Imitation and Poetry in *Republic* 10'. In J. Moravcsik and P. Temko (eds), *Plato on Beauty, Wisdom and the Arts*. Totowa, NJ: Rowman and Littlefield, 1982, 47–78.

Rosen, S. *The Quarrel between Philosophy and Poetry: Studies in Ancient Thought*. New York: Routledge, 1993.

Skillen, A. 'Fiction Year Zero: Plato's *Republic*'. *British Journal of Aesthetics* 32, No. 2 (1992), 201–8.

Stewart, J. A. *The Myths of Plato*, ed. G. R. Levy. Fontwell, Sussex: Centaur Press, repr. edn, 1960.

Tate, J. '"Imitation" in Plato's *Republic*'. *Classical Quarterly* 22 (1928), 16–23.

Tate, J. 'Plato and "Imitation"'. *Classical Quarterly* 26 (1932), 161–9.

Urmson, J. O. 'Plato and the Poets'. In J. Moravcsik and P. Temko (eds), *Plato on Beauty, Wisdom and the Arts*. Totowa, NJ: Rowman and Littlefield, 1982, 125–36.

Other Works Cited

Aristophanes *The Acharians, The Clouds, Lysistrata*, trans. Alan H. Sommerstein. Harmondsworth: Penguin, 1973.

Aristotle *Ethics*, trans. J. A. K. Thomson. Harmondsworth: Penguin, rev. edn, 1976.

Aristotle *Poetics*. In *Classical Literary Criticism*, ed. and trans. T. S. Dorsch. Harmondsworth: Penguin, 1965.

Aristotle *The Politics*, trans. T. A. Sinclair (rev. by T. J. Saunders). Harmondsworth: Penguin, rev. edn, 1981.

Berlin, I. 'Two Concepts of Liberty'. In *Four Essays on Liberty*. London: Oxford University Press, 1969, 118–72.

Burke, E. *Reflections on the Revolution in France*. Harmondsworth: Penguin, 1968.

Carr, E. H. *What Is History?* Harmondsworth: Penguin, 1964.

Collingwood, R. G. *An Essay on Philosophical Method*. Oxford: Clarendon Press, 1933.

de Beauvoir, S. *The Second Sex*. Harmondsworth: Penguin, 1972.

Derrida, J. 'Signature Event Context'. In *Margins of Philosophy*. Chicago: University of Chicago Press, 1982, 307–30.

Descartes, R. *Meditations on First Philosophy*, trans. John Cottingham. Cambridge: Cambridge University Press, 1986.

Ferrari, G. R. F. 'Plato and Poetry'. In G. A. Kennedy (ed.), *The Cambridge History of Literary Criticism*, Vol. I, *Classical Criticism*. Cambridge: Cambridge University Press, 1989, 92–148.

Friedan, B. *The Feminine Mystique*. Harmondsworth: Penguin, 1965.

Frosh, S. *Identify Crisis: Modernity, Psychoanalysis and the Self*. London: Macmillan, 1991.

Green, T. H. 'Lecture on Liberal Legislation and Freedom of Contract'. In *Works*, Vol. III. London: Longmans, Green & Co., 1900, 365–86.

Hegel, G. W. F. *Hegel's Introduction to Aesthetics: Being the Introduction to the Berlin Aesthetics Lectures of the 1820s*, trans. T. M. Knox. Oxford: Clarendon Press, 1979.

Hegel, G. W. F. *Logic: Encyclopaedia of the Philosophical Sciences*, Part I, trans. William Wallace. Oxford: Clarendon Press, 2nd edn, 1892.

Hegel, G. W. F. *Philosophy of Nature: Encyclopaedia of the Philosophical Sciences*, Part II, trans. A. V. Miller. Oxford: Clarendon Press, 1970.

Hegel, G. W. F. *The Philosophy of Right*, trans. T. M. Knox. Oxford: Clarendon Press, 1942.

Hobbes, T. *Leviathan*, ed. J. Plamenatz. London: Collins/Fontana, 1962.

Hume, D. *Treatise of Human Nature*, ed. L. A. Selby-Bigge. Oxford: Clarendon Press, 1888.

Huxley, A. *Brave New World*. London: Granada, 1977.

Jones, S. *The Language of the Genes: Biology, History and the Evolutionary Future*. London: Flamingo, 1993.

Kant, I. *Critique of Pure Reason*, trans. Norman Kemp Smith. London: Macmillan, 1929.

Kant, I. *The Critique of Teleological Judgement*. In *The Critique of Judgement*, trans. J. C. Meredith. Oxford: Clarendon Press, 1952.

Kant, I. *Groundwork of the Metaphysic of Morals*. In *The Moral Law*, trans. H. J. Paton. London: Hutchinson, 3rd edn, 1961.

Laing, R. D. *The Politics of Experience and The Bird of Paradise*. Harmondsworth: Penguin, 1967.

Lenin, V. I. 'A Great Beginning'. In *Selected Works in One Volume*. London: Lawrence & Wishart, 1969, 478–96.

Locke, J. *An Essay concerning Human Understanding*, ed. A. S. Pringle-Pattison. Oxford: Clarendon Press, 1924.

MacIntyre, A. *After Virtue*. London: Duckworth, 2nd edn, 1985.

Marcuse, H. *One Dimensional Man*. London: Routledge & Kegan Paul, 1964.

Marx, K. *Capital*, trans. Samuel Moore and Edward Aveling. Moscow: Foreign Languages Publishing House, 1961.

Marx, K. 'Critique of the Gotha Programme'. In *Selected Works* (2 Vols), Vol. II. Moscow: Foreign Languages Publishing House, 1958, 13–37.

Marx, K. *Grundrisse*, trans. Martin Nicolaus. Harmondsworth: Penguin, 1973.

Marx, K., and Engels, F. *The German Ideology*, Part I, ed. C. J. Arthur. New York: International Publishers, 1970.

Mill, J. S. *On Liberty*. In *Utilitarianism and Other Writings*, ed. M. Warnock. London: Fontana, 1962.

Mill, J. S. *Utilitarianism*. In *Utilitarianism and Other Writings*, ed. M. Warnock. London: Fontana, 1962.

Nietzsche, F. *The Birth of Tragedy: Out of the Spirit of Music*, trans. Shaun Whiteside. Harmondsworth: Penguin, 1993.

Nietzsche, F. *Twilight of the Idols and the Anti-Christ*, trans. R. J. Hollingdale. Harmondsworth: Penguin, 1990.

Norris, C. *Derrida*. London: Fontana Press, 1987.

Popper, K. *The Poverty of Historicism*. London: Routledge & Kegan Paul, 2nd edn, 1960.

Rorty, R. 'Deconstruction and Circumvention'. In *Essays on Heidegger and Others. Philosophical Papers*, Vol. II. Cambridge: Cambridge University Press, 1991, 85–106.

Rousseau, J. J. *The Social Contract and Discourses*, trans. G. D. H. Cole. London: Dent, 1913.

Sartre, J.-P. *Being and Nothingness*, trans. Hazel Barnes. London: Methuen, 1957.

Sayers, S. *Marxism and Human Nature*. London: Routledge, 1998.

Sayers, S. 'Mental Illness as a Moral Concept'. *Radical Philosophy* 5 (1973), 3–8.

Sayers, S. *Reality and Reason: Dialectic and the Theory of Knowledge*. Oxford: Blackwell, 1985.

Sekora, J. *Luxury: The Concept in Western Thought, Eden to Smollett*. Baltimore: The John Hopkins University Press, 1977.

Smith, A. *The Wealth of Nations*. Harmondsworth: Penguin, 1970.

Szasz, T. S. *Ideology and Insanity: Essays on the Psychiatric Dehumanization of Man*. London: Calder and Boyars, 1973.

Weber, M. *The Protestant Ethic and the Spirit of Capitalism*, trans. Talcot Parsons. New York: Scribners, 1958.

Wilde, O. 'The Soul of Man under Socialism'. In *De Profundis and Other Writings*. Harmondsworth: Penguin, 1973.

Index

Plato's *Republic*